THE BIG THREE
MOUNTAIN-
MOVERS

THE BIG THREE MOUNTAIN-MOVERS

TRUST
DELIGHT
COMMIT

JIM BAKKER

with Robert Paul Lamb

LOGOS INTERNATIONAL Plainfield, New Jersey

Jim Bakker

Trust in the Lord, and do good; so
shalt thou dwell in the land, and
verily thou shalt be fed.
Delight thyself also in the Lord;
and he shall give thee the
desires of thine heart.
Commit thy way unto the Lord;
trust also in him;
and he shall bring it to pass.

Psalm 37:3-5

Table of Contents

1

The Big Three Mountain-Movers

The liberating message of *The Big Three Mountain-Movers* represents the most important instruction God ever breathed upon my life. It absolutely changed Jim Bakker—my personality, my outlook on life, my ministry.

Through this message, God took a shy and timid boy from Muskegon, Michigan—a boy filled with deep-seated feelings of inferiority—and allowed him to have a part in evangelizing the world for Jesus Christ.

From my own experiences over the last sixteen years, I know there are mountains in people's lives they feel just can't be moved—mountains of financial debt, physical defects and sickness, mental pressures, and frustrations.

Sometimes these mountains just seem to grow and grow and grow until you want to wring your hands in despair and scream. People have frequently asked me, "What can ever deliver me from these mountains I continually face?"

If you have found yourself with that question on your lips, then you are an excellent candidate for this liberating message. Moving mountains can become a way of life for you. Problems will no longer stop you. If fact, you will rejoice in the midst of difficulties knowing that God is about to perform another miracle in your life. I have seen this happen in my own life. I've seen it happen with others. I've seen it daily through the ministry of PTL. The message of the Big Three can revolutionize your life.

Some of you may already be thinking I'm painting an awfully rosy picture. I'm not. There will always be problems. Until we're home in heaven with Jesus you can count on difficulties and obstacles in your life.

But as children of God, you and I can overcome the problems that seek to plague our lives. We can move mountains. That was the way the Lord Jesus Christ did things and after all, He said we would do even greater things than He did (John 14:12).

God's perfect will for His children is "that thou

mayest prosper and be in health . . ." (3 John 2). It is clearly not the will of God for His children to be sick. If your body is sick, God wants to heal you. He wants you well.

It is not the will of God for His children to be poverty-stricken. If you're in need of money, God wants to prosper you. If you've never met Jesus Christ as your Lord and Savior, He wants to save you. The Bible declares over and over that God is vitally interested in mankind. Specifically, God is interested in you!

If you have a mental picture of the Lord being some cantankerous old man with a long, white beard sitting around the portals of glory dreaming up ways to make your life miserable, get that idea out of your head. That's a complete and total lie of the devil.

God loves you! He sent His only begotten son, the Lord Jesus Christ, to die for you. He wants to bless you. He wants you to become an overcomer, a mountain-mover. That's His perfect desire for you. The abundant life Jesus preached is available for you.

As you read this book, I want you to constantly remember God loves you. He's concerned with you as a person. You are a very important consideration in the kingdom of God. If you read this material on the Big Three with the understanding that God loves you, your life can be changed. You will never be the same again.

Discovering the Big Three

Back in 1969, during a frightful experience in my life, I began discovering the principles of *The Big Three Mountain-Movers*. I had what could possibly be called a nervous breakdown. Doctors identify that condition as occurring when your nerves prevent you from working and that's essentially what happened to me.

For four consecutive years, I had handled two live television shows a night over the Christian Broadcasting Network. The long hours and constant pressures finally caught up with me one night after I got home. As I tried to rest in bed, wave after wave of dizziness swept over me and my stomach erupted in continual vomiting.

For the next month, I stayed home. I couldn't even stand to have people come around me. My nerves were so raw just taking a shower felt like hundreds of tiny needles were pricking my body. I couldn't sleep. I felt as though I was losing all the restraints that held my life together.

The doctor gave me medication to end my dizziness but the medicine caused my kidneys to fail temporarily. Tranquilizers were prescribed for my nerves. Instead of calming me down, the pills made me worse. I felt as nervous as the proverbial cat on a hot tin roof.

I was only twenty-nine years old at the time. "You're too young to be having serious problems with nerves," the doctor reminded me.

I knew the doctor was right but my problems wouldn't go away. Some of my problems loomed completely out of proportion to their actual size. I feared that what little control I had over myself might snap at any minute. If that happened, I was finished, maybe even ready for a mental ward somewhere.

I prayed seemingly without any results. I had prayed for thousands of people over television and they were healed. Now I needed a healing and couldn't get one. God seemed not interested in Jim Bakker.

Watching television one day during this time, I saw an interview with Dr. Claire Weekes, a medical doctor from Australia, who specialized in nervous disorders. A deeply committed Christian, Dr. Weekes talked about faith in God being one of the greatest cures for nervous problems.

"When you find yourself getting tense over some problem, don't fight to keep calm," she suggested. "Simply accept your condition and imagine yourself floating on water or a fluffy cloud."

As Dr. Weekes spoke, it was if God himself were speaking. She described perfectly the situation I had been going through. I had thought I was the only person on the face of the earth with those horrible symptoms.

Dr. Weekes explained the clue to healing for general nervous problems was in four simple steps; facing the problem, accepting it, floating, and letting time pass. Almost immediately I could see that what she was saying connected with the Scriptures I had been studying that week.

The Scriptures were found in Psalm 37:3-5: "Trust in the Lord, and do good; so shalt thou dwell in the land, and verily thou shalt be fed. Delight thyself also in the Lord; and he shall give thee the desires of thine heart. Commit thy way unto the Lord; trust also in him; and he shall bring it to pass."

When you commit something, you give it up. You don't fight. Inside, I felt as if God was saying He wanted me to let go of my problems. He wanted me to surrender my problems to Him.

I noticed Deuteronomy 33:27 tied in exactly with the Scriptures from Psalm 37. It reads, "the eternal God is thy refuge, and underneath are the everlasting arms." Instead of floating on water or a cloud (as Dr. Weekes suggested), I began picturing myself floating in the arms of the Lord.

Part of my road back to recovery was in recognizing I had a problem which I couldn't solve myself. But where my abilities to solve problems ended, God's abilities began.

Dr. Weekes had said to face the problem. Being a Christian, I could take her suggestion a step further. I could face the problem and give it to God. Using Psalm 37:3 as the basis, I knew I could trust God to solve my problem. Surely He has the answer to all of man's problems. After all He had said to Jeremiah, "I am the Lord, the God of all flesh: is there any thing too hard for me?" (Jer. 32:27).

Beyond that, since the Lord already had the answer for the problem, in faith I could begin praising Him for it. That's what Psalm 37:4 suggests. As I did that, I could expect the desires of my heart to be met. In this case, my desire was to be healed.

Releasing the problems to God meant they were no longer mine. That's where Psalm 37:5 fit perfectly. Commit means to give up, surrender or release, and that's what I did. I released the whole situation to Him. Finally I could rest in God (Ps. 37:7). I could relax. I could let time pass, which was another step according to Dr. Weekes's method.

As I began to put these principles to work in my life, the Lord began giving me some practical suggestions to follow. These practical things became steps of faith for my healing.

The first was exercise. Because of my job's long hours, I had neglected to properly exercise my body. Since the law of sowing and reaping (Gal. 6:7, "whatsoever a man soweth, that shall he also reap") works negatively as well as positively, I had reaped sickness.

For years I had misused my body. And the consequence of breaking one of God's fixed laws like sowing and reaping was predictable. It ended in breakdown!

The next step was nutrition. My work schedule had made it difficult to eat properly, so I had just snacked. Now the Lord instructed me to begin eating a balanced diet.

Lastly, I needed diversion. All of my life had been wrapped around serving God through television. Yet there was no time left to go aside and get my interests balanced and my life more well-rounded. So I began taking time to fish leisurely and reflect on my priorities.

As I began to grow stronger physically and as my mental fitness began to return, I sensed I had stumbled across a dynamic principle of God in Psalm 37:3-5. I felt the Scriptures represented an untapped source of power and blessing which God was making available to His children.

If this simple principle of "trust, delight, commit" could work with my nerve problem, couldn't it also work with other problems in life? What if I needed a job? Or what about supplying money? Did this mean "trust, delight, commit" could be applied to financial, physical and mental problems? Somehow I believed it could.

A Personal Word to You

Doctors report that in the United States alone there are over a million people who are afraid to leave the safety of their homes. Many people cannot even run to the corner grocery store without experiencing great stress. Others are gripped by strange fears of the darkness, of meeting new people, of heights or depths, or fears of being alone.

I have been down many of these roads myself. I know these fears are real. They are genuine to many people. Hospitals and institutions are filled to overflowing with people who simply could not cope with the pressures and frustrations of life.

But there is hope, both for you and for me. It is found in the person of Jesus Christ. He cares for you. He alone is the answer to your need. He alone can set you free.

If you have experienced problems with your nerves, if you've struggled to keep a tight hold on life, if you've suffered from fear—whatever your problem might be—I want you to trust God for the answer to your problem. I want you to believe God has the answer and that particular answer is available to you. Right now!

If you're ready to hand your problem over to the Lord, join me in this prayer:

Heavenly Father, I have this problem. (Now tell the Lord exactly what your problem is.)

Father, I know you have the answer for this problem. I trust you to solve it. I praise your holy name for the answer which is on the way. I give the problem totally over to you. I will not worry about it again. I will not fret and fume. I will forget it. I will rest in you. I ask this prayer in the name of Jesus Christ. Amen.

Now that you have prayed, I want you to continually thank God for the answer. Remember, you have given your problem to the one who loves you the most. You have committed your problem to the one who is most concerned about your life. Now continually walk in His love.

2

Principles
of the Big Three

"TRUST in the Lord, and do good; so shalt thou dwell in the land, and verily thou shalt be fed. DELIGHT thyself also in the Lord; and he shall give thee the desires of thine heart. COMMIT thy way unto the Lord; trust also in him; and he shall bring it to pass." (Psalm 37:3-5)

Although David writes Psalm 31 as an old man (verse 25, "I have been young, and now am old"), he is still pondering what seems to be the injustice and circumstance of life. Is that something you've ever done? I know I have.

In times past, I've looked at people who were living in open sin yet appeared to be enjoying the goods things of life as much as any dedicated

11

Christian. Frequently I've wondered "how can these things be?"

David gives us an answer to this question in Psalm 37. With the perspective of time, he realizes it's not how you start out in life but how you finish. He apparently has seen many people prospering in spite of wickedness. But in verse 2 he points out these people won't always continue in their good fortune, "For they shall soon be cut down like the grass, and wither as the green herb."

Therefore, he gives these three commands: trust, delight, commit. With each command comes a promise. If you want to dwell in the Canaan land of promise, be fed and enjoy the good things of life, don't follow the example of the wicked and chase after their life styles. Simply trust and delight in God and commit your way to Him.

The desires of the heart will be granted only to those who delight in the Lord. When a person delights in the Lord, their desires become purified so God can grant their requests.

The act of commitment brings to pass the justice which seemingly has been delayed. As it says in Psalm 37:6, "He shall bring forth thy righteousness as the light, and thy judgment as the noonday."

God Wants You to Trust Him

In the Old Testament, there are seven Hebrew words translated "trust," which itself occurs 155 times. "Trust" is the New Testament word for "believe." The Hebrew word for "trust" in Psalm 37:3 is *batach* which means to confide in, so as to be secure and without fear. This word appears in 107 passages of Scripture.

I've found if you really trust God you can have confidence in Him. God won't fail you. You can absolutely rely on Him and His word. You know that God isn't going to pull the rug out from under you.

I know the fear that runs through people's hearts. Sometimes they think if they dedicate their child to God, the Lord will take that child. I've known young people who feared giving their lives to Christ because they erroneously thought God would send them off as missionaries to the darkest reaches of Africa.

God is not trying to spoil your life. He loves you. He is simply trying to bring each of us to a point of surrender to His master plan for our lives. Job had obviously found that place. In spite of all the trouble and woe that fell upon him, Job was able to say, "Though he slay me, yet will I trust in him" (Job 13:15).

Many people recall the rich young ruler who came to Jesus seeking to follow the popular Galilean. Knowing where the young ruler's true interest lay, Jesus said, "Give up all that you have and follow me."

The Scripture records in Mark 10:22 what the

rich young ruler did. "And he was sad at that saying, and went away grieved: for he had great possessions."

Some people think if the rich young ruler had obeyed Jesus he would have been forced to live in poverty. A few actually teach poverty as a way of life. I don't know any place in the Bible where it states poverty is spiritual. All Jesus was trying to get from the rich young ruler was a total commitment.

In that same passage of Scripture Jesus declares, "There is no man that hath left house, or brethren, or sisters, or father, or mother, or wife, or children, or lands, for my sake, and the gospel's, but he shall receive an hundredfold now in this time . . . and in the world to come eternal life" (Mark 10:29,30).

Anytime I see people giving to God, He is always multiplying it back, sometimes a hundredfold. That's what the Scripture declares. The Bible does not teach poverty as a way of life for Christians.

Look how God provides for His people. "But my God shall supply all your need according to his riches in glory by Christ Jesus" (Phil. 4:19). How will God provide? He says the measure will be "according to his riches in glory."

That leads to the inevitable question, "how rich is God in glory?" Revelation 21:18-21 gives the following description of the New Jerusalem where the Lord resides:

"And the building of the wall of it was of jasper: and the city was pure gold, like unto clear glass.

"And the foundations of the wall of the city were garnished with all manner of precious stones. The first foundation was jasper; the second, sapphire; the third, a chalcedony; the fourth, an emerald;

"The fifth, sardonyx; the sixth, sardius; the seventh, chrysolyte; the eighth, beryl; the ninth, a topaz; the tenth, a chrysoprasus; the eleventh, a jacinth; the twelfth, an amethyst.

"And the twelve gates were twelve pearls; every several gate was of one pearl: and the street of the city was pure gold, as it were transparent glass."

Your heavenly Father is rich. He is not poor. Look at these Scriptures which detail the Lord's possessions:

". . . for all the earth is mine" (Exod. 19:5).

"For every beast of the forest is mine, and the cattle upon a thousand hills" (Ps. 50:10).

"The silver is mine, and the gold is mine, saith the Lord of hosts" (Hag. 2:8).

I believe if the rich young ruler had simply trusted Jesus the situation would have been much different. If he had said, "Lord, I'm willing to give it all up. It's all yours," I believe the Lord would have given it all back, plus a hundred times more."

The first key of the Big Three is God wants you to trust Him. God wants you to know He has the answer to your problem. He knows your need. He is vitally concerned with your situation.

Who better than the King of the universe would know how to handle your problem? After all if the Creator of heaven and earth has gone to the trouble of sending His only son into the world to redeem you, doesn't it make sense He's equally concerned with your other problems?

"Are not five sparrows sold for two farthings, and not one of them is forgotten before God? But even the very hairs of your head are all numbered. Fear not therefore: ye are of more value than many sparrows" (Luke 12:6,7).

You and I can rely on God's Word. He cannot fail. He has never failed. Listen to the words of the Psalmist, who had discovered this marvelous truth about God. "As for God, his way is perfect: the word of the Lord is tried: he is a buckler to all those that trust in him" (Ps. 18:30).

John 6:29 in the Amplified Bible explains exactly what God wants from us. "This is the work that God asks of you, that you believe in the One Whom He has sent—that you cleave to, trust, rely on and have faith in His Messenger."

This is what God desires from you. Trust Him. Believe He has the best in store for you. God has not called us to do something unattainable. If Jim Bakker with all his fears, insecurities and doubts can do it, so can you! "He that overcometh shall inherit all things . . ." (Rev. 21:7).

God Wants You to Delight in Him

The Living Bible's version of Psalm 37:4 reads, "Be delighted with the Lord. Then he will give you all your heart's desires."

In his best-selling book, *Power in Praise,* Merlin Carothers draws special attention to this verse. Says Carothers:

> Notice the order of importance here. We don't make a list of our heart's desires and then delight ourselves in the Lord in order to get them. We're first to be delighted, and once we've experienced being really delighted with God, we'll discover that everything else becomes secondary. Still, it is true that God does want to give us all our heart's desires. Nothing short of that is His wish and plan for us.
>
> If we could only learn to be delighted with the Lord in everything first!"

When a person begins to delight in the Lord, it becomes so natural to freely praise Him. Nehemiah tells us "the joy of the Lord is your strength" (Neh. 8:10). God has a reason behind us delighting in Him—we can keep spiritually strong.

Most of us easily start out delighting in God but then a problem crops up and our disposition turns sour. That's exactly when we should remain joyful and still be delighting in God.

The prophet Habakkuk records just such a terrible situation in Habakkuk 3:17. "Although the fig tree shall not blossom, neither shall fruit be in the vines; the labour of the olive shall fail, and the fields shall yield no meat; the flock shall be cut off from the fold, and there shall be no herd in the stalls." Yet in the face of this, Habakkuk declares in verse 18, "Yet I will rejoice in the Lord, I will joy in the God of my salvation."

You can do the same thing in your own life. When things go wrong, you can turn to Romans 8:28 and see why Christians can be delightful in adversity. "And we know that all things work together for good to them that love God, to them who are the called according to his purpose."

All things work together for good. Not just part but all. That includes the problem you're facing right now. That includes the situation that's hounding your life. Because we have learned to trust God, we can praise Him for all things working in our lives.

Praising God in all situations is not easy. It goes against all of man's intellect. It just doesn't make sense. But then again, none of God's ways make sense to the natural man.

I grew up in a church from a major Pentecostal denomination. A denomination that prides itself on proclaiming the full gospel. Yet, I found that very few of the people knew how to praise God outside of a church service. Many times I wanted to praise God, I felt like my jaws were wired shut. Praise was bottled up within me.

Praising or delighting in God is simply an act of the will. I can either choose to praise God, or I can sit around with the problem on my shoulders and choose not to. Most people—Pentecostals or not—don't know how to praise God outside of a church service.

What happens to people who don't learn to praise God? Deuteronomy 28:47,48 gives a sober warning. "You will become slaves to your enemies because of your failure to praise God for all that he has given you."

What happens to people who are always grumbling and complaining? If they're sick, they stay sick. They may even get worse and die. Why? Because they have failed to praise God. They have actually become slaves to their enemies—sickness, poverty, death and all the rest.

The Bible teaches that Jesus has redeemed us from the curse of sin, sickness and poverty. How can evil dwell within us if we are praising God? It can't. Praise will drive off the enemies of your soul. It is a weapon given to Christians by our heavenly Father.

It's the same when somebody talks wrongly about you. Defending yourself, you decide to fight back by slandering them. In the process you have become a slave to them. Jesus said, "all they that take the sword shall perish with the sword" (Matt. 26:52).

The children of Israel wandered in the desert for forty years. Why? Because they grumbled and complained. God parted the Red Sea for them. They were fed from heaven. Yet they still grumbled. As a result one whole generation of them never entered the promised land.

God has a promised land of blessings for many of us but we will never enter until we learn to delight ourselves in Him. The blessings are available. They are within reach. But to receive them you must follow His instructions. Praising and delighting in God are all part of your marching orders as Christians.

Before his calamity, Job was a wealthy man. But during his time of trouble, Job did not sin with his lips (Job 2:10). Afterwards, the Scripture records "the Lord blessed the latter end of Job more than his beginning" (Job 42:12). In short, the Lord doubled everything Job had before. That's a measure of God's great love and blessing to His children. It was true in Job's day. And today.

The Hebrew word *anag*, which is translated as "delight," means to be soft or pliable. God wants His children to become pliable and moldable in His hands.

The second key of the Big Three is God wants you to delight yourself in Him. When you begin delighting in God, you're saying, "God, whatever you want, I want. I give you total charge of my life." As you confess that statement to God, a new joy will flow into your life. Along with that joy will come a sense of power and strength. It will push you into a new dimension of mastery over the problems of life.

God Wants You to Commit Yourself to Him

Psalm 37:5 says, "Commit thy way unto the Lord; trust also in him; and he shall bring it to pass." The third and possibly most important key of the Big Three is God wants you to commit your way to Him. In this case, the word "way" means everything!

When you give your money or jewelry to a bank for safe-keeping, they put it in a safety deposit box and lock it up in a big vault. The bank is holding these items in trust for you. That's exactly what God wants us to do with our problems. He wants us to deposit them with Him.

God wants us to entrust Him with each and every situation we face. If we trust in this way, He gives us a promise: "he shall bring it to pass." That's your dividend from the Lord. He will solve the problem.

The word "commit" has various meanings: give in charge, trust, surrender. Almost every victory in my life came when I told the Lord, "I give up." In fact, we almost titled my life story, "I Give Up" instead of *Move That Mountain!* Winning by giving up is contrary to man's plans, but it works with God.

In 1972 when I left an important position with the Christian Broadcasting Network, I had no idea the Lord had plans to create the PTL Television Network. When I left CBN, I was simply following the direction of the Holy Spirit.

The night of our farewell at CBN, I walked out of the building wondering, "What am I going to do now?" The future was unknown. All I knew was that I was following God.

In time, following God meant conducting telethons around the country and temporarily hosting another Christian talk-variety program in Los Angeles. But ultimately, Tammy and I came to Charlotte and the "PTL Club" was born. Today, the PTL Television Network is the largest purchaser of television air time outside the three major networks, ABC, NBC and CBS.

Would PTL have become a reality without such a commitment on my part? I seriously doubt it.

Proverbs 3:5,6 gives a picture of the committed life. "Trust in the Lord with all thine heart; and lean not unto thine own understanding. In all thy ways acknowledge him, and he shall direct thy paths."

In my case, I didn't know the path was leading to Charlotte and the founding of the PTL Television Network. All I did was commit myself to the Lord and follow Him as doors opened or closed. In doing that, God's perfect will was accomplished.

Because of my original obedience to the Lord, I am now able to see thousands of persons come to a saving knowledge of Jesus Christ plus countless others baptized with the Holy Spirit and healed. The fruits of this just seem to grow and grow and grow with the Spanish version of the PTL Club already on the air and our Japanese and Korean versions soon to begin.

The Hebrew word for "commit" is *galal*. It means to roll on or wallow in. When you commit a problem to God, then you can roll or wallow in His goodness. You've abandoned yourself to Him. The whole problem now belongs to God.

This sense of giving up or abandoning yourself to God works in many practical ways. When Tammy and I first came to Charlotte, we had planned to be here for only a few days. But during the telethon I was conducting, God moved in a miraculous way. People were saved by the hundreds, cancers dropped off bodies and tumors vanished.

Just like a voice in the night, the Holy Spirit said, "Jim, what more do I have to tell you to do than to make your home base in Charlotte?"

"No more, Lord," I answered. "You don't have to say anything else. I believe you. Your anointing is here and I want to be where your anointing is."

Immediately I flew back to California to sell our house. I was a little concerned about the house because Tammy had hung pictures everywhere. Not just a few pictures either, she had hung picture galleries. You walked into the house and an entire wall was covered with pictures. Since houses show much better with the furniture in place, I was praying for a quick sale.

The Lord answered that prayer and the house sold in three days. I flew back to Charlotte. The staff packed up our furniture and moved it to our new house in North Carolina.

Two months later when the sale was supposed to close, I got a telephone call. It was a real estate man in California. "Reverend Bakker," he said unhappily, "the deal on your house fell through."

It was a bombshell. The news hit me like a wet towel smack in the face. "Oh, Lord," I moaned, thinking about the empty house and the walls full of holes as if some wild machine gunner had raked it. "I'll never make it now," I said dejectedly.

Right at that instant I wanted to wallow in self-pity.

Fortunately Tammy was standing nearby. "Wait a minute," she said sharply. "You've been preaching that once we've committed a problem to God, we ought not to take it again. You've got to practice what you preach."

Immediately, I knew she was right. Faith leaped back up in my heart. Here was a beautiful chance for commitment to work in an emergency. I knew it would either work or I would be faced with the costly prospect of paying one house payment in Charlotte and another in California.

Tammy and I prayed. "Lord, we commit this problem to you. If that house doesn't sell and if we can't make the payments, we might have to go to the poorhouse but you're going with us. This is your problem and we give it to you."

That night, we went to bed and slept like babies.

Twenty-four hours later, I received a call from California. The house had been resold for several thousand dollars more than I had paid for it. Commitment had won again!

Once you've committed a situation to God, rest your case with Him. It's like a case being tried in court. After the pros and cons of a case have been explained before a judge the case is rested. Then the jury brings its verdict. That's exactly what you're doing with your problems. Rest your case with God. Let Him bring the answer to pass. Let Him bring the solution to you.

Don't Stall the Answer—Commit

Many times even after we've committed that nagging problem to God, the answer somehow seems stalled. There are occasions when you've told the Lord the problem was His, yet within moments you were still mentally working the situation out. Does that sound familiar?

Sometimes commitment has to be a moment-by-moment experience. Otherwise things like anxiety, worry and fear can stall the answer. Problems can easily entangle you unless commitment becomes a life style, a way of living to you.

"Casting all your anxiety upon him, because he cares for you," says the Scripture in 1 Peter 5:7 (NAS). The word "cast" means to throw like tossing a ball. If we actually trust Jesus, then it's time to throw Him the ball. Throw the problem to Him.

Keep your eyes on Jesus even as you commit the problem to Him and look for the answer from Him. Hebrews 12:1 (NAS) gives us some sound advice for handling our nagging problems of stalled commitment. "Let us also lay aside every encumbrance, and the sin which so easily entangles us, and let us run with endurance the race that is set before us, fixing our eyes on Jesus, the author and perfecter of faith."

3

The Big Three,
Korean-Style

Discouraged and frustrated, Pastor Yong-gi Cho was ready to leave the ministry in the late 1950s. Yet today he pastors the world's largest Pentecostal church, the Full Gospel Central Church in Seoul, South Korea, which has 47,000 members.

The 47,000 members are told to attend church only once on Sunday, because the $2.5 million church building seats only 10,000 people. Four services are held each Sunday.

Dr. Cho, the church's thirty-eight-year-old pastor, has a staff of 72 paid and 1,300 unpaid pastors and 100 additional ministerial assistants. The church has an annual budget of $2 million, owns more than $20 million worth of real estate including 300 condominiums, an apartment house, a distribution center and office complex, a gymnasium, and a "prayer mountain" visited by 200,000 last year. All of this in a country where the average income is $700 a year.

The church building itself sits next to the South Korean House of Parliament on Yoido Island in the Han River. The building is air-conditioned, acoustically perfect, and supports a dome that rises five stories above the main auditorium.

The church's varied activities range from Sunday school which uses 3,000 teachers to early morning prayer meetings to midweek leadership training seminars on closed-circuit television. It also sponsors 40 missionaries and has a goal of sending some 500 missionaries around the world.

Recently Pastor Cho was my guest on the PTL Club. During the interview, he began expressing his formula for how the world's largest Pentecostal church was built. Simply put, Pastor Cho said the formula involved asking God, seeing yourself with your request, and speaking the word of creation.

Immediately, as Pastor Cho spoke, I could see his three keys of ask-see-speak tied in directly with trust-delight-commit. Pastor Cho even talked about giving in the same manner as I see it, and expressed a spiritual principle that works in South Korea as well as America because it is based on the Bible.

Here is the substance of Pastor Cho's interview. I call it "Practicing the Big Three, Korean-Style."

Jim: Dr. Cho, your church is already the largest in the world. Do you plan to expand your facilities to hold more than 10,000 at a time?

Dr. Cho: Right now my church seats about 10,000 people at one time but we are expanding since we expect to have 58,000 people by the end of this year. This last year we added more than 10,000 new Christians so we are building an addition which seats about 4,000.

Jim: Has your church started other churches?

Dr. Cho: Yes, this is my third pastorate. I am with the Assemblies of God and we have about 350 churches and 200,000 members in South Korea right now. About one fourth of those churches are my branch works.

Jim: And yet, your church keeps growing?

Dr. Cho: Right. I follow the Bible principle which says if you give more, God is going to pay more back.

Jim: That's marvelous, because I know pastors, if they had members going off to another church, they would almost have a heart attack. And yet you encourage your members to start another work and God doesn't take away from your church. He continues to bless it.

Dr. Cho: This is kind of like planting seed. If you

29

seed more, then you are going to harvest more. So if you give Christians to other churches, then you are going to get more. Anyway I want to have more sinners coming to my church. Saints I'm willing to share. Sinners I want more of.

Jim: I hope all of the pastors in the United States are listening right now. You wonder how to get people into your church. Give some of the old members away. But it's God's fixed law of sowing and reaping, giving and receiving.

Dr. Cho: Many people think about exercising their faith in just financial matters but the same principle works in the saving of a lost soul. You give today. Tomorrow you get. So I am exercising the same law of faith in my church. Usually every Sunday, we add about two hundred new converts. So we give about two hundred or three hundred members a week to another church.

Jim: What caused your church to become the largest in the world?

Dr. Cho: Some people think churches start in a particular location. I believe the church starts in the heart of the minister. First, you must have the vision and a basic faith in God. If you really believe you are going to have a big church, you will have it. I always believed I would build the largest church in the world even when I was in Bible school. So the church started out of my heart.

I actually applied three laws. First, you must ask God. Second, you must see the answer in your vision. Third, you must speak the word of creation. In my heart twenty years ago when I was a fledgling minister right out of Bible college, I knew I was going to have the largest church in the world. I prayed that to the Lord. I saw it in my heart. I claimed it. I spoke it.

The Bible says in Genesis 1:2,3, "the Spirit of God moved upon the face of the waters and God said. . . ." If you don't speak the word, nothing happens. You speak and creation comes.

Jim: Dr. Cho, this is some message. I'm so excited to hear you say these things today.

Dr. Cho: Well, some ministers are developing all kinds of programs to build churches. In Korea we are simply applying the law of faith. If you apply the law of faith, like energy, it goes out and creates. Not by human energy, but this is done by the power of the Holy Spirit and by the power of faith. I am actually staying out of my country for six months each year but I am still carrying out my ministry there. By faith, I can do it from a hotel room anywhere in the world.

Jim: You make it sound so simple.

Dr. Cho: It really is.

Jim: What Dr. Cho is saying can apply to every person's life, to every home situation, to every business matter. He said, you ask, you see and you speak.

Dr. Cho: That's right. You see the finished product. Then you must speak the word of creation. You do it so the Holy Spirit will have something to work with. Today people are not giving the Holy Spirit something to work with. They are only begging. We read in the New Testament no place where Jesus Christ ever begged. He simply gave the word. His disciples did the same thing. Peter and John said, "Silver and gold have I none but what I have I give. Rise and walk." When Moses was at the Red Sea, he was crying out to God. The Lord said, "Why do you call out to me? Let the sea be divided."

There may not be time enough to pray but there is always time for us to give the word of God. When we are praying at home, we should pray through, that is until we know we have the answer. But once we have the faith, then it is time for us to give the word. God is the God who raised the dead and called things which be not, as if they were. So to walk with God, you must call those things which be not as if you already had them.

Jim: How did all of these concepts work in your church?

Dr. Cho: In 1969 when God told me to build this church, I had eight thousand members, He spoke to me one day while praying, "Son, you go right in front of the Congress Hall, buy the land and build a church which seats ten thousand people. Then send missionaries throughout the whole world." When I found out the cost of the project—$2.5 million—I said, "God, you must have chosen the wrong person. I'm not that kind of man." But you know, you can't argue with God. So I went to the elders' board and told them the situation. They asked how much money would I raise from America. I said, "None." They shook their heads. Next, I went to the six hundred deacons. When they heard the situation, they all dropped their heads.

I came back to the Lord saying, "The elders and deacons won't stand with me. What do I do now?" God spoke very quickly to me. "When did I ask you to go to the elders and deacons? I said for you to build the structure. That was a command." It was then I knew I had no choice. So I believed God, applied the law of faith and in less than five years, I received $2.5 million in cash through contributions. The church is debt-free.

Jim: You are gone over half the year, yet the church still operates successfully. How does your cell ministry help that operation?

Dr. Cho: Most people want to belong to big things, but evangelism is done through the small cell. Right now, I have twenty-six hundred deacons. These people are my associates. They are lawyers, housewives, technicians, businessmen. They are trained, unpaid ministers. I also have the city of Seoul divided into two thousand cells. One cell usually consists of eleven to fifteen families. They have home meetings which some of the neighbors attend. Some people won't go to church but they will go next door for a visit. There they have prayer, instruction and fellowship. One of the reasons churches don't have revival is that so many people are flowing into the church, and flowing right back out. But once people come into my church, they are put into a cell group. They can't leave the cell unless they move to another town. Cell leaders are constantly calling them, feeding them, encouraging them.

When the cell grows beyond fifteen families, it splits and another cell starts. It's like a biological cell split. You see the large cathedrals of the world are empty because they are centered around a personality. But my church is decentralized. I'm not indispensable. I'm dispensable. If I'm there, the church grows. If I'm gone, the church grows. Any time God wants to take me away, the church goes on. If the communists ever hit our city, they could dig up the whole town and not find all of the cell groups.

Jim: What part has the Holy Spirit played in your church growth?

Dr. Cho: More than seventy percent of our people have received the baptism of the Holy Spirit. He is the one who sends revival. Every moment I try to recognize Him in my ministry. He is my senior partner so I am supposed to cooperate with Him. Without His power, we can do nothing. As soon as people get saved in our church, we encourage them to receive the Holy

Spirit at the cell meetings.

Jim: In discussing your principles of asking, seeing, speaking, this is just good basic communication with God, isn't it?

Dr. Cho: Yes. In my personal prayer life, I am always applying the law of asking and thinking. Many people are just asking and asking and asking. The Bible says in Ephesians 3:20 that God "is able to do exceeding abundantly above all that we ask or think." Scripture exhorts us to think. Many times our prayers are hindered because we don't have clear-cut thinking.

When I pray, I bring my thoughts into subjection to His thoughts. And the Holy Spirit begins to bring God's thoughts to my thoughts. I pray by thinking the request. This is as much a law as Einstein's are.

When I started my church, I used a large American army tent. At the time, I asked the Lord to give me a table, a chair and a bicycle. I prayed and I really believed. I waited five months and I still hadn't received. So I was depressed and discouraged. I said, "God, I know you are telling me the truth but if you wait too long and give those things after my death what profit will I get out of them?" I cried for some while and then I felt a tranquility in my spirit. The Lord spoke to me, "Cho, I answered your prayer five months ago." I said, "But Father, I didn't receive those things." He said, "That is the mistake many of my children are making. You've been asking for a table, a chair and a bicycle. But don't you know there are different kinds of tables, chairs and bicycles? What chair? What table? What bicycle do you want?"

A Scripture came to my mind. It was Hebrews 11:1, "faith is the substance of things hoped for. . . ." Things. Clear-cut things. "If you have vague things, I can't answer," God said. "Get clear-cut things in your mind. Think of it, then order." I said, "Father, I'm sorry. I cancel all of those past prayers." I tried to think clearly of what I wanted. A table made of Philippine mahogany. A chair with an iron frame and rollers on the bottom so I could move it around freely. And a bicycle made in the U.S.A. Everything was so clear-cut. Then I asked in such a way God could not make a mistake with those things. I received each one of those items.

Since that time, I do not pray in vague terms. It's useless. When Jesus was on His way to Jericho, a blind man came up to Him. Jesus asked, "What do you want?" Everybody knew he was coming to be healed but the Lord wanted to hear the specific request.

Jim: I know what you're saying is true, Dr. Cho. God wants us to pray specifically for what we have need of. A lot of people have the mistaken notion, if you're praying for a house or a car, God is supposed to deliver the car to the driveway and drop the new house on the front lawn. But we need to go out and find the item we want. Then speak the word of faith. Claim the thing your faith will allow.

Once I claimed a house about $20,000 beyond my means. I didn't know the right price because the real estate people had told me incorrectly. I had gone and claimed a doctor's home, and I was just a little old preacher. I wasn't making a doctor's income, but standing in the house, I told the real estate people, "I will take this house." We claimed it. Later the real estate people confessed the mistake. But somehow God had put the faith in my heart. I said, "It makes no difference. We want this house." We moved in and God supplied every dime we needed.

Why Dr. Cho Succeeds

In talking with Dr. Cho, I found the foremost reason for the success of the Central Church in Seoul. He always preaches the Bible. His sermons are made up entirely of expositions from Scripture. So when people come to church, they don't come to hear him. They come to hear what God is saying through him out of the word. He knows the word of God is a greater word than his own personal word. This, of course, is a central theme of practicing "The Big Three Mountain-Movers."

SEE Your Need Met—Now!

The same day Dr. Cho appeared on the PTL Club he prayed for our vast television audience. I felt a mighty anointing of the Holy Spirit in that prayer, so I am including it here especially for you. As you read over this prayer, I want you to lift your own personal need before God and claim it met. See yourself with the answer. See yourself healed.

You can speak destruction in your own life, or you can speak healing, encouragement and health. Speak the word of faith as you read this prayer.

"Our heavenly Father, we come to you in the name of Jesus Christ. Right now, we bind our hearts to you and we loose the power of the Holy Spirit in our lives.

"Heavenly Father, we agree together according to your mighty word. We plead the blood of Jesus Christ over our lives. We see ourselves touched, healed and met with our requests and needs. We speak the word of healing. We speak the word of victory. We speak the word of the answer.

"We are healed in the name of Jesus Christ. We receive the answer. We receive the victory. We receive all of this in the name of Jesus Christ and for His glory. Amen."

4

Putting the Big Three to Work

I'm sure many of you are saying, "It's fine for Jim Bakker to be able to practice commitment. Being president of the PTL Television Network, he needs to practice it. But what about me? I love the Lord too. Can't I follow God in the same way?"

The answer is an absolute YES!

Commitment is for every child of God, not just for television evangelists with million-dollar operating budgets.

You can practice commitment. Here's how. Suppose you have a problem in your home. Maybe you've got a problem on the job, or you're facing a big financial test. Maybe it's just that you and your wife can't agree. Perhaps the kids are creating problems.

The first thing you need to do is understand that God has the solution to your problem. No matter how big the problem, or how small, God has the solution. The only way you will be able to get that problem solved is to commit or surrender it to God.

That means you no longer have to think about it. Remember the Scripture says, "For as he thinketh in his heart, so is he" (Prov. 23:7). If you're thinking about the problem, you're still holding it. Give it to God.

This also means you don't talk about the problem any longer. Remember the Scripture says, "He shall have whatsoever he saith" (Mark 11:23). If you're talking about the problem, you still haven't committed it to God. Don't dwell on the problem, dwell on the solution.

People are constantly walking up to me wanting prayer for difficult situations in their lives. Just recently I was in a meeting in Charlotte. A short, plump woman with a harried expression on her face walked up after the meeting.

"I'm so nervous, I can't sleep at night," she moaned, tears glistening in her eyes. "My home's falling apart. The kids don't mind anymore. My husband is always gone. The situation is going from bad to worse. I just don't know what I'm gonna do."

"Excuse me, excuse me," I said, trying to

interrupt her to pray.

"Oh, I haven't finished telling you my problems yet," she responded in surprise.

The more she talked the worse I felt. By the time she finished telling me all the juicy, ugly details of her problem, I was about finished myself. It seemed like a negative spirit had actually walked into the room.

Very seldom do I ever see people with an attitude like this woman receive answers to prayer, no matter who is doing the praying. People like her seem to be in love with their problems. Perhaps they wouldn't have anything to talk about if they didn't have this problem.

Look what the Scripture says about such talk. Proverbs 18:7 says, "A fool's mouth is his destruction, and his lips are the snare of his soul." Proverbs 18:21 repeats almost the same thing: "Death and life are in the power of the tongue."

Jesus even talks about the power of words in Matthew 12:37. "For by thy words thou shalt be justified, and by thy words thou shalt be condemned."

Once you surrender a problem into the hands of God, you are believing He is big enough to handle your situation. In effect you are saying, "God, you are the creator of heaven and earth. You put the moon and stars in place. If you are not big enough to handle my problem, who is? I trust you and I know you are more than capable of handling this problem. Here is the problem."

When you give your problem to the Lord, simply picture yourself mentally laying that problem at the feet of Jesus. That problem now belongs to Him. It is His property.

You don't have to dwell on the problem anymore. You don't have to run around looking for solutions to it. This problem belongs to the Lord. Now God will bring a solution to pass. He may use you or He may use someone else, but he will solve the problem in His way.

The Voice of the Devil

One of the things you need to be aware of is the voice of the enemy, which will be constantly whispering words of worry, discouragement and defeat in your ears right after you've committed the problem to God. The devil knows that once you master the art of committing a problem to God, you are then less susceptible to any of his tricks.

We know from the Scriptures that God speaks in a "still, small voice." That's a description of the Lord's voice as found in 1 Kings 19:12 when God spoke to Elijah after he had fled to a cave to escape Jezebel's threats to kill him.

But just as God speaks in a still, small voice, the devil has a counterfeit voice. It's still and small. But it's a voice of worry and upset. The voice is always negative. It's always filled with trouble and woe. Yet in the face of all that, many Christians buy the suggestions of the devil.

The devil delights in playing mental games with people. He constantly tells you things about yourself and about other people which are not true. Jesus said one of the characteristics of the devil is that he is a liar. In fact, Jesus declared unequivocally the devil is the father of liars (John 8:44).

In John 10:10, Jesus gives us a complete picture of the devil's purpose on earth. "The thief cometh not, but for to steal, and to kill, and to destroy," He said.

What does the devil want to steal? Who does he want to steal it from?

The devil's sole purpose is to rob you of the very thing God wants to give you. He wants to destroy your health, kill your body, steal your blessings. He wants to snatch victory from you. He wants you to believe his lies. He wants you to believe God doesn't hear you when you pray.

The devil is always trying to suggest something bad is going to happen. "You are going to get some incurable disease and die," he'll tell you. "Your child will get hurt in some horrible accident."

For many years, I'd wake up late at night and great fear would come upon me. At times, I'd worry the nervous problem I had many years before was coming back. Sometimes the fear would strike me with overpowering suddennness. It seemed to come from nowhere.

But as I have grown in my relationship with the Lord, I have learned to say, "Devil, I refuse to accept this. I command you in Jesus' name to get out of here."

The Bible says to "Resist the devil and he will flee from you" (James 4:7). If you don't take authority over the devil, he will clearly claim it over you. Jesus defeated the devil in the wilderness by using the word of God on him (See Luke 4:8, 10). He told the devil, "It is written, it is written." He was simply using the word of God on His enemy. That's the clue to beating the devil. Use the word of God on him.

Once you begin hearing all the mental suggestions "God won't help you" or "commitment is impossible to practice," you simply order the devil to leave you in Jesus' name. You refuse to buy any of his suggestions. You refuse to listen to his lies.

Another good method I've found for chasing the devil off is to begin praising the Lord. That's where delighting in the Lord (Ps. 37:4) comes into the picture. There is nothing the devil hates more than a Christian walking around praising the Lord. But on the positive side, there is nothing God loves more than to hear His children praising His name.

Act on Your Commitment

In many cases once you've committed a problem to God, the Holy Spirit may give you some instructions to put your faith to work. Remember, faith without works is dead. In fact, J.B. Phillips translates James 2:17 to read, "Faith without the right actions is dead and useless."

A few verses later, Phillips says, "Faith without action is as dead as a body without a soul." By the same token, commitment without action is dead.

Look at the story of the poor widow in 2 Kings 4:1-7. She was penniless and the creditor was going to take her two sons as slaves. All the woman had was a pot of oil. But obeying the directions of Elisha, the woman borrowed pots of her neighbors and God filled each one with the oil. The oil didn't stop until there were no more pots to fill.

Above all, the widow acted out her faith. Each step she took in following the prophet's directions was a step of faith. Her faith was active.

Many people on our staff have frequently asked me, "Jim, please pray for me to get a house. We don't have any money but we'd still like to have one."

Any time I hear comments like that I always make the same suggestion. "If you feel like God wants you to have a house or anything else, you go out and pick out what you want. Only the people who actually go out to pick a house are the ones who usually get one."

All of that may sound like an extremely simple statement but going out to find a house is actually faith in action. It's an act of trusting God for a house.

Don Storms and Sam Orender, two members of the PTL staff, are perfect examples of how God provided houses. Although the Lord provided the houses in different ways, both men acted out their commitment which is the key to the Big Three.

When Don and his wife Ruth joined the PTL Club, they wanted a house in Charlotte but didn't have any money. They heard the message on commitment and decided to go looking for a house anyway. They found a house bordering the Heritage Village. In fact, the property's back yard touched the PTL property.

In faith, Don planted a small vegetable garden on the PTL land but directly behind the property he had claimed. He called it his "faith" garden. Unexpectedly, money came for the house's down payment and the Storms family moved in. The garden produced a bountiful crop as well.

On the other hand, Sam and Kathy Orender looked without success for a home. The Orenders had never owned a home and were a little frightened at the prospect of claiming a house that would put them in debt for years.

"I can't afford it," Sam continually told me. "I

don't know how I would pay for it if I had a house."

"If you want a house," I told him firmly, "commit it to the Lord and He will take care of it."

Unable to find a house to their liking, Sam and Kathy located a builder who agreed to construct a custom-built house with no contract. "I'll build it," the man said. "If you like it, you can buy it. If not, you don't have to."

Sam and Kathy claimed the house and watched it go up. They continually took people to see the house under construction. All the while, they praised the Lord for His gift of the house. Within six months, the house was finished and they had managed to save eight hundred dollars.

The builder agreed to handle the complete down payment for the Orenders allowing them to pay a small amount each month. They even lived in the house a whole month without paying a dime. Once again, the Lord had provided. "Trust-delight-commit really works," Sam Orender says. "It works in many areas of life."

You may be in one of those situations like the Orenders and the Storms. You don't have any money but you want a house. How can you find God's perfect will for you to have a house? Have you actually been out looking at houses?

The Bible tells us in part of our theme Scripture (Ps. 37:4) "He shall give thee the desires of thine heart." How do you even know the desires of your heart until you have actually looked?

Many people just pray, "God, please give us a house." I don't regard that as much of a prayer. I've found God wants us to be specific in our prayers. He wants us to tell Him what our desires are.

What Is Your Level of Faith?

When you present a teaching on God's abundant provision, some people will go out and attempt to buy a lot more than they need. About such, the Bible says, "Ye ask, and receive not, because ye ask amiss, that ye may consume it upon your lusts" (James 4:3).

I'm not talking about foolishness here. I'm talking about faith, and one of the things you find out about faith is there are different realms or levels of faith.

At PTL, we've bought over a million dollars worth of television equipment and paid out about five million dollars more on the Heritage Village. It's important to recognize I didn't start out on a level of faith working with millions of dollars. I started out by believing God for a newer car than the one I was driving. I started out believing God for a nicer apartment than I had. Then I moved up.

Decide on what you need. Is it a house? A solution to a problem? A healing? Money? Salvation of a loved one? Maybe you just want to lose weight.

The Bible tells us clearly we can have "whatsoever we say." So you begin by simply speaking out what you need. You do that from an honest, open heart. Then, you begin thanking and praising God for the answer.

I have seen God work some unbelievable miracles in supplying the needs of His people when they step out in faith. One of our pledge partners, a builder and his wife who lived in upstate New York, lost everything a few months ago through a series of devastating business deals. They had exactly $3.46 left.

Days before, they had heard me talking about commitment over PTL, so they decided to commit everything they had to God. They decided to give three dollars to PTL and eat their last meal on the forty-six cents. I can't imagine what they could find to eat that cheaply but they did.

It wasn't very many hours after they had committed those three dollars into God's trust that the builder received a signed contract to construct buildings in excess of $150,000. Praise God!

In some instances, God has to completely revamp our thinking before we move ahead in a life of commitment. Some people think you needed plenty of money in the bank before you can begin to operate in faith. I never have. PTL had no collateral when we began the Heritage Village project. All we had were some rented studios and faith in God.

Faith is not something you can reason out in your mind. Hebrews 11:1 defines it as "the substance of things hoped for, the evidence of things not seen." Faith is something you hope for but can't see. But faith is also substance.

Moffatt's translation of Hebrews 11:1 reads, "Now faith means that we are confident of what we hope for, convinced of what we do not see." The New English translation says, "Faith gives substance to our hopes. . . ."

Intellectually, it's almost impossible to explain faith. It's like trying to comprehend the love of God. Who can fathom the depth, heighth and breadth of our heavenly Father's love?

You Must Begin Somewhere

As you begin your venture in commitment, perhaps you feel unable to believe God for a new home, a new car, or even a better-paying job. Perhaps that's not your level of faith. Maybe all you want is a healing for your body. Great!

Let's begin somewhere. That's most important. You must begin somewhere. Once you find that level of faith, you will discover yourself growing stronger every day in your relationship to Christ. The Bible clearly shows different levels of fruitfulness. ". . . some a hundredfold, some sixty, some thirty" (Matt. 13:23).

Maybe you'll be starting off at a level of thirty or sixty instead of a hundred. That's fine. The important thing is to *start!*

The Bible is filled with accounts of people who came to Jesus and received their requests. The centurion's servant was healed (Matt. 8:5-13). Two blind men received their sight (Matt. 9:27-30). The leper was cleansed (Mark 1:40). The woman with an issue of blood was healed (Mark 5:25-34). The beggar, Bartimaeus, was healed of blindness (Mark 10:46-52).

Notice one thing about all six of these people. They all came to Christ and asked. They took action. The centurion walked to meet Jesus. The two blind men cried out as Jesus walked by. The leper beseeched Jesus. The woman touched the hem of the Lord's robe. Bartimaeus cried out with a loud voice. All of these people acted out their faith.

Remember God Loves You

Remember God loves you. He is concerned with you. ". . . for he careth for you" (1 Pet. 5:7). You are the object of His attention. God wants to bless you. He wants your life to be filled with peace and joy.

". . . Ask, and ye shall receive, that your joy may be full" (John 16:24). The time to start is now. The life of commitment is one of the greatest adventures you'll ever know as a Christian.

Join me.

5

The Big Three
Overcome Sorrow
and Grief

". . . For your Father knoweth what things ye have need of, before ye ask him" (Matt. 6:8). This is one of the remarkable truths about God. Even before you pray, He knows everything you need. And even better, He has already made provision in His word for you.

Within each of our lives come moments or darkness, times of despair, hurt, and sorrow. It seems no one is exempt from such. At times, it appears as if these struggles will never end.

But once again, God has made provision for His children. Isaiah 61:1-3, in the Living Bible, tells us: "The Spirit of the Lord God is upon me, because the Lord has anointed me to bring good news to the suffering and afflicted. He has sent me to comfort the broken-hearted, to announce liberty to captives and to open the eyes of the blind. He has sent me to tell those who mourn that the time of God's favor to them has come, and the day of his wrath to their enemies. To all who mourn in Israel he will give:

"Beauty for ashes;

"Joy instead of mourning;

"Praise instead of heaviness."

Quoting from these very Scriptures, Jesus added in Luke 4:21, "These Scriptures came true today!" The Lord was drawing attention to himself, saying He was the one who would bring the good news to people suffering, broken-hearted, afflicted. He would take the sorrows of their lives and give them beauty, joy and praise. What a great plan of exchange!

Jesus is the great cure for the sorrows and troubles of your life and mine. He has come to set you free from these afflictions. "He healeth the broken in heart, and bindeth up their wounds" (Ps. 147:3).

In practicing the Big Three, it is important to consider Romans 8:28 when sorrows, problems and troubles come into our lives. The Living Bible says, "And we know that all that happens to us is working for our good if we love God and are fitting into his plans."

All that happens. That includes the sorrows, the

problems and the troubles. Even those things are going to turn out for good, if you love God and are following Him.

2 Corinthians 4:17 makes a similar promise. The Living Bible says: "These troubles and sufferings of ours are, after all, quite small and won't last very long. Yet this short time of distress will result in God's richest blessing upon us forever and ever!"

A Testimony of Trusting God

Mrs. Betty Joyce Obert of Cottondale, Florida, has a testimony of trusting God which best exemplifies what I'm saying about trusting God in the face of troubles, problems and sorrows. It never fails, because God's word can't fail.

My husband, Donnie, and I grew up together in Marianna, Florida. We both quit high school in 1962 to get married. Donnie worked at a service station at first, and almost immediately, the babies started coming along. Donna was born in 1963, John in 1964, Brenda Sue in 1966 and Tobby in 1971.

Both of us had gone to church off and on as children, and I professed to be a Christian at one time, but neither of us were currently living for Jesus. Naturally, a marriage without Jesus presents many problems and I honestly didn't know how much longer it would last.

During the summer of 1973, I told Donnie I had to go back to church and get my life straightened out. I wanted him to go back with me. He agreed at first but after going once he quit. I continued going to church and June 25th I repented of my sins and asked God for His forgiveness. The peace, joy and love I had once known now came back.

Everything seemed to improve at first, but then Donnie wanted to make a change. At the time, he was working on shrimp boats at St. Augustine, Florida, but he wanted to go back to Marianna and become a truck driver again. For over a month Donnie drove a truck while I prayed that God would bring him back to St. Augustine and his family.

One night in prayer, the Lord spoke to me. "If you will just keep living for me and put me first in your life, I will save your husband."

Almost immediately, I began responding, "Lord, I thank you for saving him." I had no problem believing God was going to do exactly that.

Donnie returned home in a few weeks but he had yet to give his life to Christ. In fact, he continued drinking heavily and spent many nights out, coming home in the wee hours of the morning.

Halloween night came and Donnie's

company was holding a party. The children and I went to church that night while Donnie went to the party. He didn't return home until about two o'clock but with the Lord's help I was able to be sweet and kind to him. For some unexplainable reason, Donnie never went out drinking after that.

For the next month, our home life was filled with happiness. Both of us were excited to know another baby was on the way. The weekend before Thanksgiving several members of Donnie's family came to visit. That Saturday morning, we spent sightseeing in St. Augustine. Donnie was working but took the afternoon off.

About two o'clock, Donnie, his brother, and our children, John and Tobby, took our boat and went water skiing. They left word for us to meet them at Jackson's Landing to fry fish for supper.

I arrived at the landing about four o'clock. Our truck and trailer were there but nobody else was in sight. We decided to go ahead and set up everything for supper. By nightfall, they still weren't back and I was getting worried. I knew Donnie never stayed out this long on the water even though he knew how to handle a boat and was a good swimmer.

Finally, we went to a nearby store and called the police. They came quickly, asked many questions and called the Coast Guard. A search began immediately. Inside, I worried about my two boys, ages nine and two. I feared they might be cold and wet and it deeply troubled me.

Sunday morning, an ice chest was found floating on the water, and I began to have more hope that everything was okay. Monday, they located a boat seat and the next day a guide rope and one life jacket was found. Wednesday, they found the bodies of my husband and my two children.

It was almost a living hell for the four days when I didn't know if my husband and children were living or dead. But through those days, I recognized a strength that seemed to be flowing from within me. A strength that brought peace to my troubled heart. And that strength was greater than the sorrow and grief I was experiencing. I knew that strength and peace was Jesus Christ.

There was a possibility my husband had enough insurance to pay for all the funeral expenses but as it turned out there was no insurance money at all. I was faced with paying several thousand dollars. I didn't know anything to do but trust God. I was a widow, now almost three months pregnant, with two other children and owing money for my three loved ones' funeral.

Somehow God worked a miracle. People who knew about the tragedy began sending contributions to me and all of the money was paid. On top of that, I didn't have a moment's trouble with the baby and on June 6, 1974, another little boy was born. I named him Joey.

Almost three years after the accident, a shrimper caught his net on the motor of our boat mired deep in the St. John's River. A wide slice was found in the front of the boat. The police theorized the boat had struck an obstruction in the water turning it over and drowning my husband, his brother and our two children.

Almost four years have passed since the accident. There are many things about the tragedy I don't understand. I don't pretend to understand them. But one thing I do know. I know the Lord saved my husband as He promised He would.

The Lord never promised how or when He would save Donnie. He just said He would. People who identified Donnie's body said he apparently had both children in his arms when they died. There was *time* for him to have accepted Christ.

Many times the devil has tried to make me doubt this but I know God does not make a promise and then refuse to keep it. He always keeps His Word. I know my husband and children are with Jesus today.

During the month Donnie was away from home, I committed him to God believing and trusting that God would save him. I believe that God did exactly that. But beyond the promise of saving Donnie, I have seen how trusting God overcomes every sorrow, every heartache, every bit of sadness. It has even filled that aching void left in my life.

In the face of this tragedy, I have found that trusting God is the only answer to the problems and perplexities of this life. I wouldn't be happy and at peace today without it.

It wasn't until just a year ago I first saw the PTL Club and heard Jim Bakker's message on the Big Three Mountain-Movers. But when I heard it, I realized, "This is exactly what I was able to do with my husband's salvation. I had trusted God to save him. I continually thanked and delighted in God to do just that. And I totally committed my husband in God's hands.

God Makes Provision for You

If you are facing some kind of time of sorrow, there is hope for you in God's Word. God has made provision for you there. 2 Corinthians 1:3,4 in the Living Bible says:

What a wonderful God we have—he is the Father of our Lord Jesus Christ, the source of every mercy, and the one who so wonderfully comforts and strengthens us in our hardships and trials. And why does he do this? So that when others are troubled, needing our sympathy and encouragement, we can pass on to them this same help and comfort God has given us.

The Lord has made provision for you to have His peace in a time of turmoil. The very peace, Mrs. Obert spoke about in her testimony, is yours for the asking. Philippians 4:6,7 in the Living Bible says:

Don't worry about anything; instead, pray about everything; tell God your needs and don't forget to thank him for his answers. If you do this you will experience God's peace, which is far more wonderful than the human mind can understand. His peace will keep your thoughts and your hearts quiet and at rest as you trust in Christ Jesus.

God has also promised you comfort in the times of loneliness, or when you are faced with walking through a dark valley. Isaiah 41:10 in the Living Bible says:

Fear not, for I am with you. Do not be dismayed. I am your God. I will strengthen you; I will help you; I will uphold you with my victorious right hand.

The Bible is absolutely filled with provision for you in every situation you face. Here is a sample of the ones I have found:

Strength in a time of temptation—James 1:12-16 and 1 Corinthians 10:6-13.

Courage in a time of fear—Hebrews 13:5,6 and Ephesians 6:10-18.

Protection in a time of danger—Psalm 91 and Psalm 121.

Relief in a time of suffering—2 Corinthians 12:8-10 and Hebrews 12:8-10.

Guidance in a time of decision—James 1:5,6 and Proverbs 3:5,6.

Rest in a time of weariness—Psalm 23 and Matthew 11:28,29.

Promises for Those Who Trust in God

Beyond the provision already mentioned, God has also made allowance for those people who trust Him. This is a special category of believer who simply takes God at His word. Notice these Scriptures:

2 Samuel 22:31: "As for God, his way is perfect;

the word of the Lord is tried: he is a buckler to all them that trust in him."

Psalm 31:19: "Oh how great is thy goodness, which thou hast laid up for them that fear thee; which thou hast wrought for them that trust in thee before the sons of men!"

Psalm 32:10: "Many sorrows shall be to the wicked: but he that trusteth in the Lord, mercy shall compass him about."

Psalm 34:22: "The Lord redeemeth the soul of his servants: and none of them that trust in him shall be desolate."

Proverbs 29:25: "The fear of man bringeth a snare: but whoso putteth his trust in the Lord shall be safe."

Isaiah 26:3: "Thou wilt keep him in perfect peace, whose mind is stayed on thee: because he trusteth in thee."

Jeremiah 17:7: "Blessed is the man that trusteth in the Lord, and whose hope the Lord is."

Nahum 1:7: "The Lord is good, a strong hold in the day of trouble; and he knoweth them that trust in him."

Psalm 125:1: "They that trust in the Lord shall be as mount Zion, which cannot be removed, but abideth for ever."

Live One Day at a Time

I've heard it said there are two days in every week in which we shouldn't worry. One of the days is yesterday with all its mistakes, troubles and sorrows. It's gone. It can't be called back. The other day is tomorrow. It hasn't arrived yet. We don't know what it will hold, so there is no need to think about it.

That leaves only one day—today. Jesus called special attention to today. He said, "Don't be anxious about tomorrow. God will take care of your tomorrow too. Live one day at a time" (Matt. 6:34 TLB).

A Prayer for Your Life

Physical pain. Heartbreak. Sorrow. Emotional trauma. These are all prices we must pay for being members of the human race. Yet, as members of another race—the children of God—we know there is victory over the struggles, doubts, fears and temptations of life.

1 Corinthians 10:13 says, "There hath no temptation taken you but such as is common to man: but God is faithful, who will not suffer you to be tempted above that ye are able; but will with the temptation also make a way to escape, that ye may be able to bear it."

God has made a way of escape for you, no matter what the problem.

If you are facing some dark struggle today, if you are facing a deep valley that looks as if it has no end, if you are lonely and discouraged, join me in this prayer to God. He has the answer to your need. He knows your situation. He is able to help you.

Heavenly Father, I come to you in the name of Jesus Christ. Lord, you know the situation I am facing just now. (Tell God exactly what the situation is.)

God, I know and I confess it makes no difference what my problem is. You already have the solution. I know that, God, because your word says so. I am standing on my authority as a believer in Jesus Christ today and trusting you to work out this problem. I delight in you and I thank you for the answer. And I give this problem totally to you. I believe the problem is solved, the need met, the answer given.

In Jesus' holy name, Amen.

Giving—
An Explosive Force

Giving is the explosive force that puts your faith or commitment into action. Commitment and faith are interrelated in many respects. Faith without works is dead, according to James 2:17. By the same token, commitment without giving is dead.

You haven't actually committed a problem to God until you give of yourself, your time, your talents, your substance. Your giving becomes a seed planted which God multiplies back. "Now he that ministereth seed to the sower both minister bread for your food, and multiply your seed sown, and increase the fruits of your righteousness." (2 Cor. 9:10).

Every time I see problems developing at PTL or

I begin to feel the pinch financially, I look around to see what I can give away. In fact, it was the gift of a large mobile trailer from PTL to another ministry that helped move us into our incredible building program.

The trailer had been bought to be used as a temporary office but the idea never worked out. For many months, the trailer sat parked outside the studios of WRET in Charlotte. I was driving to the studio one day when the Lord began speaking to me.

"I don't want you to sell that trailer," He said. "I want you to give it away." And He proceeded to tell me the ministry to whom PTL should give the trailer.

Since PTL needed the money, I began to argue with the Lord. "What about Luke 6:38?" He asked.

I thought about the Scripture. "Give, and it shall be given unto you; good measure, pressed down, and shaken together, and running over, shall men give into your bosom. For with the same measure that ye mete withal it shall be measured to you again."

If that Scripture worked for an individual, wouldn't it work for a ministry as well? Somehow I believed it could. As soon as I reached the office, I made plans to give the trailer away just as the Lord had instructed. I was looking to see what Luke 6:38 would produce.

And it happened! A fresh move of God's Spirit moved upon PTL. Hundreds more began finding Christ as Savior each month. The number of confirmed healings increased greatly. And contributions to the ministry rose dramatically.

At the time PTL had such a small outreach but I was limiting the ministry even further by not plugging into a dramatic principle of God. Once I saw Luke 6:38 would work in such a beautiful way I determined a spirit of giving would characterize every activity at PTL.

Why would I want PTL characterized by such a spirit?

Because giving is at the heart of the Big Three Mountain-Movers. It is also at the heart of Christianity. Giving is a fixed law of God. It's uniquely tied with receiving.

The Scripture says it is far better to give than to receive but Jesus pointed out in that wonderful passage in Luke 6:38 what happens when you do give. "Men shall give into your bosom." From your gift, there is a return. "Give and it shall be given unto you."

For the person who tithes his income to the Lord (that means to give one-tenth of all your income to God), look at the promise made in Malachi 3:10. "Bring ye all the tithes into the storehouse, that there may be meat in mine house, and prove me now herewith, saith the Lord of hosts, if I will not open you the windows of heaven, and pour you out a blessing, that there shall not be room enough to receive it."

What a blessing! There won't be room to hold it.

Partner's $100 Gift Produces $10,000 Return

The following letter from a PTL partner in Leland, Mississippi, demonstrates the truth of what Luke 6:38 and Malachi 3:10 promise. "Give and it shall be given unto you." The size of the blessing will be such "there shall not be room enough to receive it."

Dear Jim,

I want to share this with you and your staff. When you were building the Heritage Village, I was praying one day and the Lord spoke to me about sending $100 to PTL. He said if I would give to His building project, He would raise up a den in my house for me.

A den had been a desire of my heart for over three years. Our house was so small and we needed more room but we never seemed to be able to save any money.

In order to understand the miracle of what God did, you should know that we never tithed or gave to the church before this. So when the Lord spoke about giving PTL $100, I knew my husband would get upset. I told the Lord that but God said, "Out of his own mouth will come your answer."

My husband came home that day and I told him about wanting to give the money to PTL. Without another word he said, "Send it." Needless to say, I was shocked at his reaction.

Immediately, my husband wanted to rush out and borrow the money for the den but I asked the Lord to make the interest rates so high we couldn't afford it. That's exactly what happened.

Over the next year and a half, I praised God every day for my den. Since 'I'm a Southern Baptist, many of my friends thought I had "gone off the deep end" but I knew I had heard from God. I knew, by faith, God was going to give us a den. I had His word on the matter. The devil tried to rob me many times of God's promise but I told him I'd go to my grave believing God had spoken to me.

Since we live on a fixed income, the situation looked impossible. But over the year and a half, God provided money continually. He gave us so many financial miracles you wouldn't believe it. Excuse me. Yes, you would believe since PTL is such a miracle itself.

Today, we have a beautiful den which is almost as large as our entire house. It cost within a few dollars of $10,000. The miracle is that we paid cash for it. PTL paid cash for the Heritage Village and God beautifully allowed us the same privilege. Praise the Lord!

I know you may sometimes wonder what happens to your partners when they give out of their own needs. Truly, we can't outgive God. He always honors His Word because He is His Word (John 1:1).

I thought this testimony would bless your staff to know that God not only blesses PTL but He also blesses those partners who step out in faith and obedience to give. And the return is always greater then the seed planted. In our case, we gave or planted $100 and God returned $10,000.

Signed, a sister in Christ.

Giving Honors God

Not only does giving work in financial matter as the letter from the PTL partner in Mississip shows, but it also works in a multitude of othe ways. Pastor Yong-gi Cho, pastor of the world largest Pentecostal church, says he used the sam principle in building his church. Only in Pasto Cho's case, he gave church members to othe congregations. In the process, his church gre from 8,000 members to 47,000 members, and h expects 18,000 new converts this year!

In considering the principle of giving, I'm nc

talking about a gimmick to enrich a preacher's pocket. I'm talking about an eternal principle of God, a principle rooted in the personality and power of almighty God himself.

God is a giving God. He demonstrated His giving through the gift of His Son. "For God so loved the world, that he gave his only begotten Son, that whosoever believeth in him should not perish, but have everlasting life" (John 3:16).

Throughout His earthly ministry, Jesus Christ taught this principle of giving. Notice His words in Matthew 10:8. "Heal the sick, cleanse the lepers, raise the dead, cast out devils: freely ye have received, freely give."

During my early years as a traveling evangelist, many congregations would hold "poundings" or canned goods showers for Tammy and me. I went to many poor churches and some places this was the only form of offering.

People cleaned out the junk from their closets and shelves and brought it to church for us. The gifts were unlabeled cans of food. Some of the cans were rusty and most of the food was unfit to be eaten. This was their love gift for the visiting preacher.

The Scripture says, "Honour the Lord with thy substance, and with the firstfruits of all thine increase" (Prov. 3:9). We are to give God our best. Then we can understandably expect the best from Him.

Luke 6:38 which carries that marvelous promise about God's return for your giving also explains the measure of the return. Says the Living Bible: "Whatever measure you use to give—large or small—will be used to measure what is given back to you."

Many people don't understand why their lives aren't blessed. They try to go through the motions of being decent and respectable but nothing seems to work. Many times it all boils down to a simple refusal to obey the Scriptures when it comes to giving. Some people won't even tithe, which is basic to walking with God.

My grandmother—who has been such a great inspiration to me—always had money. Even though she worked as an hourly-paid seamstress, she never wanted for anything. Her home in Muskegon, Michigan, was paid for. Her bills were always paid on time. She served the best family night suppers.

How was a little old seamstress able to do this?

Simple. Above all, Grandma Irwin always tithed her income. Plus she always gave money over and above her tithe. She was not wealthy but she never lacked for anything. In her realm, she was blessed abundantly.

Givers Are Winners; Grabbers Are Losers!

Acts 3 records the marvelous healing story of

he lame man who sat daily at the gate of the emple called Beautiful. Seeing Peter and John about to go into the temple, the man who had been lame since birth asked alms.

"Silver and gold have I none," Peter answered, "But such as I have give I thee: In the name of Jesus Christ of Nazareth rise up and walk." The Scriptures record in Acts 3:8 that the man went "walking, and leaping, and praising God."

The life style of the child of God is giving. That was the life style of the followers of Jesus. That was he life style of the Lord himself. So Peter couldn't just ignore the lame man. He gave what he had. In his case, it was healing.

Throughout his entire earthly ministry, the Lord Jesus Christ was a giver. He constantly emphasized this theme. Notice the Scriptures on he subject. "Give to him that asketh thee" (Matt. 5:42). "Freely ye have received, freely give" Matt. 10:8).

The same attitude about giving freely was imparted from Jesus to His disciples. It is the same attitude that belongs on each of our hearts if we call Jesus Christ our Lord.

I have seen pastors hold onto church pastorates long after their time had passed to leave. Somehow they looked at their job solely as a meal ticket, a means of living. At the heart of the matter, they were afraid to trust God. They would not launch out in faith.

The result was a miserable church situation. Because the church's pastor was holding onto a meal ticket, the church was stymied. Rarely was the power and presence of God manifested in a church like that.

Walking in the Spirit is not a question of you holding onto God. It's a simple matter of you allowing God to work through you. Many of us, after years of being Christian, have yet to turn the controls of our lives over to God.

Somehow we fear being out of control if we allow a supernatural God to direct our lives. Yet, if the truth were known, the real problems in all of our lives have come because we disobeyed God and walked contrary to His plans.

Recently I read a story that presents an excellent example of what walking in faith with the Lord is like. Dave Nodar, a Catholic high school teacher, says:

One of my summer jobs, janitorial work at an elementary school, required that I use an industrial floor waxer. I had observed someone using it, and it looked very easy. But when I got behind the machine and took hold of the handles, it moved me wildly through the room. The more I struggled, the worse things got. When I finally turned it off, I was so tired and perplexed that I wanted to give up.

Another janitor, who had been watching, managed to stop laughing and show me how to work the machine. The key, he explained, was not to push it along but to let the machine move along by itself; all I had to do was balance the waxer by resting my hands on it. The machine would do the work if I would only relax and rely on its power.

Sound familiar?

Operating that floor waxer is exactly like walking with God in a commitment. God's word will work for you if you relax and rely on it. Because God and His word are the same, you are actually relying on Him. His power will take care of every situation, every problem, every need in your life.

There is a television commercial that talks about "grabbing all the gusto of life." That's the world's view of life—grabbing, fighting, holding onto, never yielding.

The Christian's view of life is giving, yielding, surrendering. Once you've done that, you can rest in God. You're no longer relying on yourself. You're relying on Him, and He can't fail!

Here's a good question to ask yourself. It's an excellent way of checking your own attitude. "Am I a giver like Jesus, or am I a grabber like the rest of the world?"

Do you have an answer?

God Wants You to Give

Did you know out of the twenty-nine parables Jesus told, fourteen of them speak about money? From the 8,000 verses of Scripture in the New Testament, 1,361 or about one out of six speaks about money, stewardship or accountability to God. That's an indication of the importance God attaches to this matter of giving.

Do you know where Jesus sat when He went to the synagogue? He sat beside the treasure (Mark 12:41). The Scripture says He observed how people gave their money.

Paul tells us in 2 Corinthians 9:7 how we should give. "Every man according as he purposeth in his heart, so let him give; not grudgingly, or of necessity: for God loveth a cheerful giver."

God cares about what you give and how you give it. Giving is a key put in your hand by a loving Father who wants to bless you. It's necessary to use that key before the door of blessing will open for you.

"He which soweth sparingly shall reap also sparingly; and he which soweth bountifully shall reap also bountifully" (2 Cor. 9:6).

Have you tried it?

Giving—God's Fixed Law

Giving is God's proven, fixed law. To Christians, it is a way of life. It's like a part of salvation. It is absolutely not some preacher's way of lining his pockets. It's a part of serving God.

Giving is a fixed principle of God. It never changes. The law of gravity is a law of God that never changes either. When the astronauts planned their trip to the moon, they had to consider the law of gravity if they expected to successfully reach their destination.

As a Christian, if you expect to succeed with God, you need to understand His principles of giving. A failure to understand these eternal, unchanging principles will hinder your progress in the Christian life.

God's law of giving and receiving is centered around Galatians 6:7, "Whatsoever a man soweth, that shall he also reap." This is a general law of God that works in every area of life.

Any farmer will tell you planting apple seeds will produce apple trees. Orange seeds produce orange trees. In the animal kingdom, like produces like. Lions produce other lions. Tigers, other tigers. Humans produce other humans.

Sowing evil produces an evil offspring. Look at the Scriptures. ". . . they that plow iniquity, and sow wickedness, reap the same" (Job 4:8). "He that soweth iniquity shall reap vanity: and the rod of his anger shall fail" (Prov. 22:8). "For they have sown the wind, and they shall reap the whirlwind . . ." (Hos. 8:7).

In the same way, giving of finances produces a financial return. Sowing seeds of love and mercy produces a similar return. "For he that soweth to his flesh shall of the flesh reap corruption; but he that soweth to the Spirit shall of the Spirit reap life everlasting" (Gal. 6:8).

Christians who don't plug into this fixed principle of God are notoriously dead and dry. So are whole churches and other Christian organizations. You can't have life without an outflow. Look at the Dead Sea as an example. It's dead because no water flows out of it.

Many Christians are like the Dead Sea. They have an inlet but no outlet. It's the attitude of the world—grabbing instead of giving. As a result, most of them have little life within.

During the middle of PTL's mammoth building program, missionary Phil Saint was a guest on the PTL Club. His brother, Nate, had been martyred in 1956 by Auca Indians, a fierce tribe in Ecuador. On the program, Phil explained how the group he headed was building a center in Argentina in honor of his late brother.

"And we need roughly two thousand dollars to finish the roof," he said.

As Phil talked, the Lord began speaking to me. "Tell him PTL will finish the building."

At first, I thought about all the debts we faced in building the new center. I almost wanted to tell

God I wasn't going to do it, but I obeyed. "Phil, we'll give you the two thousand dollars," I said.

After the program ended, I went back to my office where the day's current mail awaited me. I opened the top letter and out fluttered a two-thousand-dollar check with a note.

Once again, the Lord spoke. "Jim, you didn't really give anything away today. I am the source of all things and this is merely a transfer of funds. But you will receive the blessing of giving and obeying."

Throughout the building program—and today as well—when God says "give," I do. I obey God, knowing obedience is essential as a Christian, but also realizing the Lord will bless abundantly. This principle was demonstrated to me during construction of the Heritage Village when the Lord supplied sizable payments of $100,000, $350,000 and $487,000 to our contractor. The principle always works no matter what the amount.

How to Begin Giving—Today

It would be wonderful if everybody would automatically start giving or even tithing. But perhaps due to our background or upbringing, you have a hard time giving anything away. I know people who hoard everything. Much of it is stacked in their basements or attics. Some people have stuff stored away for thirty years or more.

If you have a hard time giving, I want you to start today. Find someone who has a need. Whether through your church, school or an organization that helps the needy, I want you to begin giving.

You might be the kind of person who won't throw anything away. "I just might use this some day," you keep saying to yourself about all that stuff.

If you have possessions (clothes, draperies, furniture, etc.) that you're not using, I want you to give it away. I don't encourage giving away junk unless it's to the city dump.

Find someone who has a need and give it to them. If possible, do if face-to-face, so you can have the joy of giving and see first-hand that it is more blessed to give than to receive.

I've recently heard there are more than forty million needy or poverty-stricken people in the United States. That's out of a total of some 200 million. If Christian people were giving according to Bible principles, there would not be a person in America in need.

Tammy and I have applied this principle of giving in our lives and we have discovered an abundance of God's blessing always coming back to us. Every time we find things in surplus around our house, we give them away.

This represents a seed sown. It gives God an

opportunity to multiply something back to us. Since God cannot multiply zero back to you, whatever you give serves as the measure. Remember Luke 6:38.

Giving is more than just finances. Some people might say I don't have any money or possessions to give away. Okay, but you've got yourself to give. You can read a book for a shut-in. You can visit the sick. You can help in church. You can baby-sit for a neighbor. There are countless ways you can practice giving by simply offering the easiest gift of all—yourself.

Not only has the Lord taught me to give financially, but He has continually emphasized the importance of giving myself to others in need. This is a vital part of the Christian life.

Back in 1975, A.T. Lawing, a charter member of PTL's board of directors and owner of an oil equipment company, came to me one day. "Jim, my sales manager has left me," he said grimly, "and the man's beginning to drain away business from my company. One of my largest customers may go over to him, and, if he does, my business is doomed. I'll go bankrupt after twenty years in business."

I tried to encourage A.T. "This is not of God," I answered. "A child of God should not have this kind of thing happen to him. We're going to do something."

A.T.'s face was still etched with concern when

he left, but I felt God was moving me to stand with this man who had done so much for others. A few days later I called the then small PTL staff together and explained the situation. We borrowed a battered, red church bus and, with David Kelton driving, some thirty of our employees went over to A.T.'s warehouse to pray.

When we arrived, A.T. was shocked that I had brought the staff with me. But he recovered in time to introduce us to all of his people and we marched into the back of his warehouse. Using a gas pump still in its carton for a pulpit, we sang hymns and had a regular worship service.

On the basis of Matthew 16:19 ("Whatsoever thou shalt bind in earth shall be bound in heaven and whatsoever thou shalt loose on earth shall be loosed in heaven") we bound the work of the devil and claimed a great victory for the Lord.

God performed an outright miracle for A.T. In spite of the fact that 1975 was a recession year marked by gasoline shortages, A.T. sold more gas pumps—250 to be exact—than anybody in the entire United States and won the manufacturer's Golden Pump Award. Praise God!

I have often wondered what would have happened if I had not obeyed the Lord and taken the staff to pray for A.T. God has many ways of working, perhaps He could have done it another way. But in this case, I obeyed and the Lord worked a miracle. The clue was in Jim Bakker taking the time, sparing the effort and giving of himself.

Maybe you have absolutely nothing to give. Okay, give of yourself and trust God to bless that. The key of giving is in your hands, but you must activate this powerful force of blessing. God wants to bless your life. He's simply waiting for you to utilize your time, your talents, your abilities for Him. I encourage you to start now.

A Prayer for You

Once a preacher was baptizing his converts in a pond. A prosperous farmer, known for his tight grip in the dollar, was wading out to be dunked. He stopped momentarily a few feet offshore and turned back.

"I forgot to take my billfold out of my pocket," he announced. "I don't want to get it wet."

"No problem," answered the preacher. "Your billfold needs to be baptized too."

Many of God's people are in the same position as that prosperous farmer. We may have been converted and baptized but our pocketbooks haven't followed suit. That requires another step of commitment—committing all that we have to the Lord. After all, we're not owners of our possessions. We're stewards of God's possessions.

That's the issue Jesus presented to the rich young ruler. That young man had kept all the commandments. He had lived a good life. Yet when faced with the ultimate step of commitment—giving up his possessions—he turned away from Jesus.

Through the example of the rich young ruler, we see a dedicated churchman, a person who knew all the rules and zealously kept them. But Jesus said the man was trusting in his riches. In fact, He said, "How hard is it for them that trust in riches to enter into the kingdom of God!" (Mark 10:24).

Paul addresses himself to the same subject in 1 Timothy 6. In verse 10, he writes, "For the love of money is the root of all evil," and in verse 17 he says, "Charge them that are rich in this world, that they be not highminded, nor trust in uncertain riches. . . ."

Riches, money, possessions. They are all temporary and very uncertain things. Jesus knew that. That's why He wanted the rich young ruler to trust in Him. God will supply money, possessions and other things, but He wants our trust to be in Him.

Some of us have been on a merry-go-round of financial problems for many years because we have not heeded the Scriptures. The prophet Haggai characterized the condition of people who have ignored God in their giving.

"Ye have sown much, and bring in little; ye eat, but ye have not enough; ye drink, but ye are not filled with drink; ye clothe you, but there is none warm; and he that earneth wages earneth wages to put it into a bag with holes" (Hag. 1:6).

If you have found yourself "putting wages into a bag with holes," you need to consecrate your earnings to God. Join me in prayer. Obey God. And watch Him do a miracle in your life.

Heavenly Father, I come to you in the name of Jesus Christ, my Lord and Savior. Father, I confess that I have ignored the Scriptures on giving. I confess I have been serving two masters. I confess I have looked upon myself as owner of my possessions. I confess my earnings have been put into a bag with holes.

Father, I ask forgiveness of these deeds and based on the promise of your word (1 John 1:9) I accept that forgiveness in Jesus' name. I know now that you remember that sin no more.

From this day forth, Lord, I commit my finances to you. I put myself, my family, everything I have at your disposal. Father, I look to you for guidance in my giving. I believe you will bless my giving according to the Scriptures. I trust you, knowing you will abundantly supply all my needs.

In Jesus' holy name, Amen.

7

Victory Over Fat through the Big Three

With millions starving to death, no nation in the world has more overweight inhabitants than America. Various estimates say there are more than 79 million fat people in America. Unfortunately, many of these people are Christians.

Fat has been the downfall of many Christians whose lives and service to the Lord Jesus Christ were shortened because their bodies had to carry extra pounds.

I've been closely associated with Henry Harrison, co-host of the PTL Club, for more than eleven years. All during this time, he has had a problem with his weight. I know how much Henry enjoys eating and I know the rich foods he enjoys. But just recently, I noticed him turning down strawberry shortcake and fruit cobbler. Then, he began losing weight. I decided to investigate. Here is the conversation that followed with Henry.

Jim: Henry, I know you've had a problem with your weight for a long time. How far back does the problem actually go?

Henry: When I was twelve years old, my mother was in Duke University Hospital for an operation. A nurse saw a snapshot mother had of me. At the time, I weighed about 170 pounds. The nurse said, "It looks like your son has a weight problem. I would suggest you have him examined by a doctor." So I was taken to a doctor. He checked my metabolism and said I had a thyroid deficiency. He then put me on thyroid pills which were supposed to help my weight problem. The pills helped some but the doctor finally decided to put me on a regular injection. I took the injections for a while and from time to time I would be placed on low calorie diets. My weight bounced up and down like a yo-yo though. By the time I was sixteen years old, I weighed 265 pounds.

Jim: Was 265 pounds your peak weight?

Henry: No. By the time I graduated from high school, I was above 300 pounds. I didn't know how far above 300 I got because that was as far as the scales registered. When I had a physical examination prior to entering college, I found I had high blood pressure. Later when I had a pre-induction physical for the army, my blood pressure was still high and I was turned down for military service. An army doctor told me, "If we were going to take that much meat into the army, it would have to be in more than one piece."

Jim: So your weight problem actually kept you out of the service?

Henry: Yes. However, I realized I had a problem and continued looking for solutions to my overweight condition. A doctor in Goldsboro, North Carolina, told me he wanted to try me on a new drug that had recently appeared on the market. The drug was a timed release capsule that contained an amphetamine. I was supposed to take one tablet in the morning and it would be released throughout the day in my body. The tablet was an excellent appetite suppressor and it worked tremendously in giving me a boost in energy as well.

Everything was fine as long as I took the tablets. I lost quite a bit of weight but when I ran out of the capsules I'd really feel low until I began taking them again. This went on for several years and every month I'd get the prescription refilled. I had never heard anything about being hooked on prescription drugs. I thought drug addiction was confined to illegal drugs like heroin or other things.

Jim: How did you come to find out this drug was actually doing your body harm?

Henry: Well, Susan and I were married in November, 1970, and about that time, the Food and Drug Administration released a report on weight reduction pills. My doctor called saying he would have to cancel my prescription until I could come in for another physical examination to justify using the medication. I decided then I wouldn't take the pills any longer. I didn't realize until months later what problems the drug had created for me. I got to the point where I couldn't make the simplest decision without going through some emotional trauma.

Occasionally we'd go out to eat and I couldn't decide where to go. Once I decided on a restaurant. I couldn't make up my mind what to eat after getting there. Susan said my disposition changed and I wasn't the person she knew before we married. It finally reached a crisis point where I had to cry out to God for help. It was only through His great grace that I was able to overcome the problem. Ultimately, I realized I had become addicted to this drug without even knowing it. Fortunately I had never exceeded the dosage, which would have created an even bigger problem.

Jim: What happened to your weight once you were off the drugs?

Henry: Naturally, my weight started coming

right back. Pretty soon I was back near the 300-pound level. That was the situation when I came to PTL about two years ago.

Jim: I know you have tried a number of diets before this. Right?

Henry: You bet. I had tried everything—the grapefruit diet, the high protein diet, the low carbohydrate diet, even fasting. I also tried leaving off certain foods.

Jim: Did you actually try losing weight through all of these methods?

Henry: Yes. I tried every plan that came along promising you a slender future. I answered newspaper ads, magazine ads, anything that promised help. Nothing ever really worked over a long period of time, though.

Jim: What conclusion were you able to draw from attempting to lose weight from all these diet plans?

Henry: I came to the conclusion I was just a natural-born fatty! At least that's what I tried to tell myself. I do know that people have different basal metabolisms. When I was a youngster, I explained away my fat by saying mother's cooking was so good. But my dad would always say, "My feet have been under her table longer than yours and it hasn't fattened me."

Jim: Did you have parents who were overweight?

Henry: Mother was a little on the stout side, but

my father was tall and never weighed more than 165 pounds.

Jim: What happened to your weight situation when you joined PTL?

Henry: I weighed about 270 pounds when I came to PTL. Over the next several months, I gained to 285. I finally said to myself, "Something has got to be done." I tried fasting and occasionally lost weight. But once off the fast, the weight came right back. Finally in December, 1976, Charles and Frances Hunter were guests on PTL. Their book, *God's Answer To Fat: Lose It!*, was the subject of much of their conversation. Frances called it, "The book that's changing the shape of America." I was really motivated by hearing the Hunters talking.

Jim: Okay, so the Hunters motivated you. But how does the Big Three fit into your story?

Henry: Well, you had preached my ordination service on the subject of the Big Three. In your message, you had put a great deal of emphasis on committing. Later I looked up the word "commit" and it means to place completely in the control of a person. Immediately I thought of an airline pilot traveling down the runway with a plane. Up to a certain point, the pilot can abort the takeoff and stop. But once past that point, he's committed. He's either going to fly or crash.

Jim: How did you relate all of this to your weight problem?

Henry: I felt like I had reached a certain point in my relationship with the Lord over my weight problem. I had struggled with the problem for years. But I felt the time had come to either commit the problem to the Lord or literally "go to pot." One of the things you pointed out in your sermon is the Hebrew word for commit means to roll or wallow. So that's exactly what I did with the weight problem. I said, "God, I can't do it so I'm giving it to you. You told me in your Word that all things are possible. You've also told me you won't violate my will. I know you can do with us only that which we will allow. Now I willingly give this problem over to you."

Before there had been times when I asked the Lord for help and He answered as long as I left the problem with Him. But once I withdrew that commitment, He took His hands off saying, "If that's the way you want to go I can't do anything else with it." I realized the weight situation was with me a long time before I ever had a close relationship with the Lord. But I knew I had to do the same thing with my weight as I had done with drinking, smoking and reading pornography. I had conquered those problems through commitment. Now I had to do the same thing with my weight.

Jim: Once you committed the problem to the Lord, what was your next step?

Henry: I went on a Daniel's fast for ten days.

That's drinking only water and eating vegetables lightly cooked without oils or butter.

Jim: Did you have a hard time with that fast?

Henry: Not really. When you're eating nothing else, even bland things taste good. Your taste buds become more sensitive. It's like when I quit smoking many years ago I realized food tasted much better. That's one of the reasons I think people gain weight when they quit smoking. However, I faced my first test of the new diet when I spoke at five different banquet meetings right after starting the diet.

Jim: How did you get past all those fancy meals?

Henry: Fancy meals is right. Instead of allowing the meals to become a stumbling block though, I used them as a means of witnessing. I told the folks at the banquets about my commitment to the Lord and whenever a dessert or something was placed before me, I pushed it away. I can say like Frances Hunter, whenever I had a temptation to eat something, I asked out loud, "Jesus, do I really need this?" And He never lies!

Jim: Did you begin losing weight right away?

Henry: Yes, I began losing weight although not drastically. But little by little, it came off and now I have lost fifty-two pounds. The Lord has helped me exercise along with losing weight so I'm keeping firm instead of just getting flabby.

Jim: What other plans did you use beside the Daniel's fast?

Henry: The Lord gave me some specific instructions to follow. I was to totally leave off bread, sweets and fats. That meant no butter or margarine too. I have been a lover of bread all my life. As a child, I was taught to eat bread. Mother sometimes fixed biscuits three times a day. I loved sweets, especially good desserts. The same thing is true of fats which Southern cooking is laced with. Having grown up on a farm, I thought you needed as much butter as bread.

Jim: I can see the Lord has taught you some new things about food with your diet. How do other aspects of the Big Three play a part in your story?

Henry: First, the Bible tells us that if we delight in Him, He will give us the desires of our heart. So the Lord has even changed my desires. Even as I'm passing up food at the table, I'm praising the Lord inside. As you know, one of my privileges at PTL is to host many of the program guests for a meal afterwards and we always have an elaborate spread. But I've learned just to pass up all the food.

Jim: What would you advise people who have had problems with their weight and just can't seem to lose weight?

Henry: The first thing they need to realize is they can't solve the problem themselves. That's part one. For me, I had to realize Henry Harrison had a problem he couldn't handle himself.

Jim: That fits right in with trusting God. In

order to trust Him, you must believe He has the answer to our problems.

Henry: I would have to say a big amen to that. I know God has the answer and nobody else has.

Jim: So you're saying even with a weight problem, a person needs to settle the issue in his heart that God has the answer to his problem.

Henry: Not only that, but God wants to make the answer available to us. He tells us in the Bible He will not withhold any good thing from us (Ps. 84:11). When Charles and Frances Hunter were on PTL, they asked everybody who wanted to lose weight to write it down. I put down the number of pounds I wanted to lose and said, "Lord, I'm giving this to you."

Jim: You told me something at the time. Right?

Henry: Yes, I said, "I've either got to lose weight or lose face." Since I had actually made my commitment on television, it would have been like bringing a reproach on the Lord if I hadn't kept my end of the deal.

Jim: What kind of reaction have you received since losing the fifty-two pounds?

Henry: I had no idea what an influence this would be on literally thousands of people wrestling with the same problem. Just recently I received a letter from a woman who said, "Brother Henry, I'm so thrilled to see that you have lost weight. I have a very dear sister-in-law who desperately needs to lose weight. I had talked to her about it and she said as long as Henry Harrison doesn't do anything about his weight I don't feel any obligation to do anything about mine. But now that you have lost weight I have convinced my sister-in-law to go on a diet using the same principle. Please don't ever let your weight come back because I need my sister-in-law and you too."

No matter where I seem to go people ask about my weight loss. Everyday before the program, when Susan and I greet the studio audience, people ask, "Brother Henry, how is your weight coming?" I always reply, "It's not coming, it's going."

Jim: So you've found the Big Three works with weight problems?

Henry: Absolutely. I trust in the Lord, knowing He has the answer. Delighting myself in Him produced getting the desires of my heart. That includes my heart's desire as well as my stomach's. The cravings of my stomach were even changed. And finally, committing the problem totally to God.

Jim: In committing your problem to the Lord, did you have to take a step to activate your faith?

Henry: Yes. The ten-day Daniel's fast launched my weight losing program. I lost around fifteen pounds during that fast. That was like a catapult in getting me moving in the right direction. But it was absolutely a step of faith like planting a seed or giving. It became a positive step which God could then bless.

Jim: How far away are you from your goal?

Henry: Presently I weigh 234. My intermediate goal is 225. I don't know where I'll go from there. Once before on a crash diet, I got down to 211. That's the lowest I've been since I was a youngster.

Jim: Crash diets usually mean a sudden weight gain once you're off the diet, don't they?

Henry: Right. Before when I lost down to 211, I didn't feel as well as I did weighing 225. But I'm confident now the Lord is going to help me arrive at a weight that is best for me. In fact, I know He is. Praise the Lord!

What Does the Bible Say about Gluttony?

According to Deuteronomy 21:20,21, gluttony ranks together with drunkenness and they both deserve the death penalty. "And they shall say unto the elders of his city, This our son is stubborn and rebellious, he will not obey our voice; he is a glutton, and a drunkard. And all the men of his city shall stone him with stones, that he die. . . ."

There are other Scriptures that speak of gluttony, appetite and self-control. Examine them with me.

Proverbs 23:1-3. "When thou sittest to eat with a ruler, consider diligently what is before thee: And put a knife to thy throat, if thou be a man given to appetite. Be not desirous of his dainties: for they are deceitful meat."

Proverbs 23:21. "For the drunkard and the glutton shall come to poverty: and drowsiness shall clothe a man with rags."

Philippians 3:18,19. "For many walk, of whom I have told you often . . . whose end is destruction, whose God is their belly, and whose glory is in their shame, who mind earthly things."

What God Is Saying Today

God is issuing a call today to the body of Christ. The call is to slim down, avoid rich foods, develop correct eating habits, discipline your body so it takes orders from your spirit (not the other way around), and heed the warning of 1 Corinthians 6:19,20. "What? know ye not that your body is the temple of the Holy Ghost which is in you, which ye have of God, and ye are not your own? For ye are bought with a price: therefore glorify God in your body, and in your spirit, which are God's."

I firmly believe God's call to the body of Christ contains the admonition to put away forever anything that would destroy the temple of the Holy Spirit. Each of us needs to consider that admonition seriously.

In calling Christian people to slim down, I'm not going to dictate how that goal should be reached. I believe the Holy Spirit will lead each person to find God's way and God's weight, and maintain it forever through prayer, discipline and exercise.

My prayer for you is simple. I pray that you open every area of your life to the inspection of the Holy Spirit. If you have a problem with discipline and self-control, ask for God's help to solve it. If you are overweight, find God's perfect weight for your body. If necessary, pray, fast and perhaps even consult with a doctor for help. If your abnormal cravings for food are demonic, seek and receive deliverance.

Above all, allow the attitude that was in Mary, mother of Jesus, to rule in your heart. "Whatsoever he saith unto you, do it" (John 2:5).

8

Hindrances to the Big Three

Circumstances are things that can be changed or may be changed from day to day in the normal course of living. But facts are hard, immovable objects that can only be changed through the direct intervention of God. Many of the situations I have faced at PTL could have only been solved through the direct, miracle-working power of God. This is fact-changing faith or what I call mountain-moving faith.

When PTL first started out to construct the Heritage Village, we didn't have the money to build a multimillion dollar center, and every circumstance seemed to indicate, "You won't make it. You can't do it."

True enough, we didn't have the actual money in our checking account. Most likely a bank wouldn't have loaned us the money. However, we did have a word from the Lord "to build."

Perhaps you're trying to believe God for the down payment on a house and your weekly paycheck is too small. Perhaps you're sick and facing a critical operation, and it is possible you might die. Maybe you have an alcoholic husband, your teenage children are becoming delinquents, and your home is falling apart.

Praise the Lord! If you've got problems like these—or even bigger—now is the time for you to begin practicing the Big Three Mountain-Movers. Now is the time to begin speaking to those mountains in your life according to Mark 11:23.

When you begin operating in the realm of commitment, you commit a problem to God no matter what the situation is. Faith doesn't consider a financial recession or a tight money market. Faith doesn't look to a miracle drug as your only hope. Faith doesn't try the route of divorce out of family difficulties. Faith looks to God for the answer.

Faith knows that God is the source of all things. "But my God shall supply all your need according to his riches in glory by Christ Jesus" (Phil. 4:19). God will supply your need. Whether that need is a new house, a healing, or the solving of a family problem, God can do it.

In the face of bleak, ominous-looking circumstances, a committed believer looks to Jesus. Instead of concentrating on the circumstances, he relies on God's word. "This problem is all yours," he tells the Lord. "I give it to you."

Then, he trusts God, the source of all things, to supply the need, to solve the problem, to bring a solution to pass.

A prime example of the word of God overcoming the facts is found in John 11, the story of Jesus raising Lazarus from the dead. The Lord Jesus Christ was carrying on His ministry when He received word that Lazarus "whom thou lovest is sick."

"This sickness is not unto death," the Lord said responding to the news, "but for the glory of God, that the Son of God might be glorified thereby."

Instead of leaving immediately for Bethany, Jesus spent another two days where He was. Even before leaving, He told His disciples, "Lazarus sleepeth; but I go that I may awake him out of sleep."

When Jesus finally arrived, He found that Lazarus had already been in the grave four days. Lazarus' sisters, Mary and Martha, each received the Lord with the same greeting. "If thou hadst been here, my brother would not have died," they said.

Jesus walked to the rock-chamber where

Lazarus lay and ordered the stone rolled away. Once again, Martha spoke up. "Lord, by this time he stinketh: for he hath been dead four days."

"If thou wouldest believe, thou shouldest see the glory of God," the Lord answered her.

As the stone was removed from the entrance to the grave, Jesus prayed a simple prayer. "Father, I thank thee that thou hast heard me. And I know that thou hearest me always but because of the people which stand by I said it, that they may believe that thou hast sent me."

Then, crying with a loud voice, Jesus shouted, "Lazarus, come forth."

And the Scripture declares in John 11:44, "And he that was dead came forth, bound hand and foot with graveclothes: and his face was bound about with a napkin."

Faith had overcome the facts!

In the building of the Heritage Village, we began during a time when we did not have enough money to complete the project. But that made no difference. "If thou canst believe, all things are possible to him that believeth" (Mark 9:23).

Jesus could have restored Lazarus "long distance" as He had the centurion's servant in Matthew 8. Instead, He came personally to the scene to demonstrate the power of God over death. And many of the Jews believed on Him.

You may just be starting out in some small step

of commitment and someone in your family remarks, "This just doesn't make sense." Remember Job's wife even suggested he curse God and die in the face of his mounting problems (Job 2:9).

Sometimes one family member has to start out alone in a life of commitment. But God is faithful even to bringing that uncommitted partner into a life of commitment. The devil will fight that harder than anything. He knows there is power in agreement.

The theme Scripture of PTL is built around agreement. "If two of you shall agree on earth as touching any thing that they shall ask, it shall be done for them of my Father which is in heaven" (Matt. 18:18).

The devil will use every possible weapon at his disposal to keep a husband and wife from agreeing in prayer. If it wasn't so powerful, the devil wouldn't fight it. Therefore, we must follow the advice of James 4:7. "Submit yourselves therefore to God. Resist the devil, and he will flee from you."

If it's not possible to agree in prayer with your husband, begin agreeing in prayer with a Christian friend. The important thing is for *two* to agree. That fulfills the Scripture and moves the hand of God.

Another Problem: Ignorance of God's Word

Another hindrance to a successful life of practicing the Big Three is an ignorance of God's word. The Scripture says in Hosea 4:6 that God's own people "are destroyed for lack of knowledge."

There are many Christians who have died from sickness and disease, yet God wanted to heal them. There are countless others living in defeat and misery because they have failed to understand what God has provided for them. Through His word, God has made provision, now and in the future, for all of His children.

Numerous times Jesus rebuked the Pharisees and Sadducees—religious people who were supposed to be schooled in the Scriptures—"for not knowing the Scriptures, nor the power of God" (Matt. 22:29).

The Lord's choice of words in the above Scripture is most fitting. I have found, in my own personal experience, Christian people who don't know God's word seldom ever know the power of God. These two facets seem to be closely related—a knowledge of the word and the power of God.

Many people have a faulty conception of God. They don't see Him as the everlasting God, the Lord, the Creator of the ends of the earth. To some, God is a combination of Santa Claus, the Easter Bunny and the Good Fairy. Even many

Christians have old, antiquated ideas about the Lord, His personality and His capabilities.

Each of us needs to allow the Holy Spirit to correct our understanding of God. Right along with that, we need to bring our daily lives into harmony with the teachings of Jesus. "Whosoever heareth these sayings of mine, and doeth them, I will liken him unto a wise man, which built his house upon a rock" (Matt. 7:24).

In my sixteen years of travel and ministry, I've met countless Christian people who seem to think there is one Bible for the preachers and another Bible for the laymen. One set of standards for the ministers and another for the common folk. One set for the Jim Bakkers of the world and another for the church members.

Wrong!

The Bible was written for all of God's children. It is an account of God's great love and provision for all humanity. Everything the Bible declares is available to all God's children—specifically, it is available for you.

One of the simplest ways to overcome this ignorance of God's word is to set aside time daily to read the Bible and pray. Choose a convenient time for yourself. Some people function best in the morning. Others in the afternoon or evening. The important thing is to do it!

Your enemy, the devil, will seek to block this time with God. Simply put, the more you understand about Jesus and His plan for your life, the more victorious you become, and the bigger threat you pose to Satan and his counterfeit plan for your life.

Jesus said the devil's sole purpose is "to steal, and to kill, and to destroy" (John 10:10). The devil seeks to rob you of God's best. He wants to kill your body. He longs to destroy your family.

In that same passage of Scripture, Jesus said, "I am come that they might have life, and that they might have it more abundantly." Abundance is a special word for God's children. It means "more than you can see any way of using." That's a measure of God's blessing. That's the kind of life Jesus seeks to give you.

A good method for studying God's word is to read a chapter of Scripture and then reflect on it. Acquire a loose-leaf notebook and write down what that particular Scripture says to you. Reflect on it.

Another way of studying the Bible is by listening to cassette teaching tapes. Each morning when I'm driving to the studio from home, I listen to them in the car. I'm seeking to bring my focus on God and His word. Therefore, when I arrive at PTL, I'm ready to go before the cameras with something fresh from the Lord. Many people who spend an hour or so driving to and from work have found it a valuable time to spend listening to an anointed teaching tape.

Whatever your own situation is, look for time

you can spend alone with God and His word. Find out what God has provided for you. Believe me, it will pay handsome dividends.

Don't Panic in the Storm!

The Scriptures recount the story of King David gathering an army to fight the Philistines. Daily he was being joined by various tribes, those of Judah, Benjamin, Ephraim, Manasseh and Issachar. Of all the tribes mentioned, there is an interesting description of the tribe of Zebulun. 1 Chronicles 12:33 says, "Of Zebulun, such as went forth to battle, expert in war, with all instruments of war, fifty thousand, which could keep rank; they were not of double heart."

The warriors from Zebulun were called "expert in war" and one of the secrets they had learned was in keeping "rank." They stayed together. They obeyed orders. They didn't panic. They were not double-minded.

Many Christians panic in the face of trouble and adversity. They break rank. Instead of looking to God when the sea of life becomes rocky and rough, many believers want to jump out of the boat. There is no question God uses these experiences to mold Christian character but many of God's people simply fail the test.

Peter stepped out of the boat in Matthew 14:29 and "walked on the water, to go to Jesus." But then something happened. "But when he saw the wind boisterous, he was afraid; and beginning to sink, he cried, saying, Lord, save me" (Matt. 14:30).

Naturally impulsive, Peter had ventured out on the water. His eyes were temporarily on Jesus, then they switched to the raging water and boisterous wind. Peter was overcome by panic and began sinking.

This picture of Peter attempting to walk on the water is like the Christian life. Many of us have become Christians and we're up on the water following Jesus. But once on the water, we've discovered there are problems. The wind blows and the water swirls around us. At times we feel as if we're sinking.

There are problems that come in the life of a Christian. But, God has made us a great promise in Psalm 34:19. "Many are the afflictions of the righteous: but the Lord delivereth him out of them all."

There will be problems. But God will deliver you from them. God will do it! You have His word on the matter.

We will all have problems as long as we live on this earth, but as children of God we can learn to be overcomers. "For whatsoever is born of God overcometh the world: and this is the victory that overcometh the world, even our faith" (1 John 5:4).

By faith in Jesus Christ, even our problems

become stepping stones to a more victorious life. That's what Christianity means—a victorious life in Christ.

The Bible describes our adversary the devil "as a roaring lion, [who] walketh about, seeking whom he may devour" (1 Pet. 5:8). Notice the word "whom." The devil cannot devour every Christian. In fact, he can't devour a single Christian whose faith is rooted in Jesus Christ.

I get discouraged and depressed at times. Many of the problems I face are mind-boggling. PTL has an ever-expanding worldwide ministry, a two-million-dollar monthly budget, over three hundred employees. I wasn't trained to be president of a television network. I'm a preacher.

Yet I'm learning every problem I face can be solved by my heavenly Father. He is more than able if I rely on Him. And besides that, God is going to bring good out of every situation I face. Romans 8:28 firmly declares that promise.

The Lord's capacity to bring good from problems is never more clearly demonstrated than in the story of Paul and Silas. The two early missionaries had gotten themselves into serious trouble. While on a missionary journey to Macedonia, they were arrested for "troubling the city." Their clothes were torn and many stripes were laid upon them. To add insult to injury, they were then thrust into the inner prison and placed in the stocks.

But at midnight, Paul and Silas prayed and sang praises unto the Lord. Notice they didn't grumble or complain. Neither man panicked. Nobody wanted to be back home with the wife and kids. Instead, they just praised the Lord.

Suddenly an earthquake erupted from the bowels of the earth, shaking the foundations of the prison. Before the story ended in Acts 16, Paul and Silas were both freed and they had led the Philippian jailer and his entire family to Christ.

The moral of this incredible story is that you can be in an earthquake without the earthquake being in you. Praise God!

Don't panic should you find yourself in the midst of a storm. Remember God is still in charge. He has never failed yet.

A Step of Faith

Another hindrance to a life of commitment lies within that nagging indecision to trust God and step out in faith. Are you currently debating over taking a step of faith in the Lord, or are you waiting until it looks safe to move?

Perhaps you're waiting until you've completely figured out the situation yourself. Why? Because we're people of reason and logic. Reason says we shouldn't act until we fully understand the situation, or until all the facts are in.

Understanding the situation or looking at the

facts can be a real problem to a Christian attempting to follow Jesus. Remember, facts don't count when you have God's word on the subject.

When God has given you a promise, all of the resources of heaven stand behind you. Since God is not a man that He should lie (Num. 23:19), you can have confidence in what He speaks to you.

Listen to what the renowned author Oswald Chambers says about confidence in God:

Rouse your soul out of its drowsiness to consider God. Fix your attention on God, on the great themes of his redemption and his holiness, on the great glorious outlines of his character, be silent to him there; then be as busy as you like in the ordinary affairs of life.

Be like the Lord Jesus; when he was sound asleep in the fishing boat he knew that his father would waken him when he wanted him. This is a marvelous picture of confidence in God.

If you are agonizing over the reliability of God's word, look to what the Lord says through the prophet Isaiah. "For as the rain cometh down, and the snow from heaven, and returneth not thither, but watereth the earth, and maketh it bring forth and bud, that it may give seed to the sower, and bread to the eater:

"So shall my word be that goeth forth out of my

.nouth: it shall not return unto me void, but it shall accomplish that which I please, and it shall prosper in the thing whereto I sent it" (Isa. 55:10,11).

The Scriptures from Genesis to Revelation are filled with the glowing accounts of people stepping out in faith, followed by God's blessing. Noah built the ark in obedience and saved his entire family. Abraham ventured into a place not knowing where he was going and became the father of nations. Joshua obeyed the commandments of God and won great military victories. Joseph and Mary saved the life of the baby Jesus by obeying the voice of God and fleeing to Egypt.

The Lord Jesus himself was the picture of obedience. As a result, the power and presence of God was continually upon His life. Healings and great miracles followed His every step.

By the same measure, the Bible clearly shows what disobedience to God's word brings. Adam and Eve were kicked out of the Garden of Eden for eating the forbidden fruit. Lot's wife became a pillar of salt by looking back at Sodom and Gomorrah, disobeying the very word God spoke. Nadab and Abihu were destroyed for offering "strange fire" before the Lord. Moses was kept from bringing the children of Israel into the promised land because he struck the rock at Meribah. Joshua lost the battle of Ai because of disobedience among the children of Israel. Saul lost his crown for not keeping the Lord's commandments, Ananias and Sapphira lost their lives for lying to the Holy Spirit.

Many of us have disobeyed the Lord by simply ignoring His words. Some have not obeyed for fear of failing. What of the embarrassment? What will people say? Many of us are chained and bound by the opinions of others.

You can be certain God never made a failure yet. He is a God of success. His word is programmed to succeed. In obeying Him, you plug into that channel of success. As His child, you can succeed.

Faith cannot be intelligently understood. After all something described as both "substance" and "evidence . . . not yet seen" is difficult to grasp. It cannot be reasoned. It is simply a deliberate act of obedience to God.

Proverbs 3:5,6 gives us encouragement in stepping out in faith. "Trust in the Lord with all thine heart; and lean not unto thine own understanding. In all thy ways acknowledge him, and he shall direct thy paths."

What will you do? Will you attempt to analyze the situation until it appears safe to proceed? Or will you act upon what God has said? The Scripture says, "Whatsoever he saith unto you, do it" (John 2:5). When Mary spoke those words to the servants of the wedding feast at Cana, Jesus turned the water into wine. Perhaps a similar miracle is in store for your life.

Is God presenting a step of faith to you? Will you obey?

If the Lord is speaking to you, how can you be sure it's God speaking? Maybe it's the devil. How can you tell the difference?

My experiences have taught me when a suggestion or a word comes from God I have a quiet urging to follow it. The urging is never screaming or shouting for my attention but it is like a "holy persistence."

Remember the Holy Spirit is always a gentleman. He never demands, condemns or berates. He is positive. He is loving. He is gentle. His leadership is never confusing because He is always in control.

The Lord's words may not sound practical—especially to the person accustomed to reasoning everything out—but they always work. Obeying God, Noah built an ark even before the first drop of rain fell. There had never been that kind of flood before. But after the ark's doors were closed, it rained forty days and nights.

God's Perfect Time for Everything

Impatience as well as failing to understand God's sense of time can be another problem while learning to practice the Big Three. God is never in a hurry to get a job accomplished. Yet He is never late either. He has a perfect sense of time.

As you begin to walk in this new life of commitment, it would profit you greatly to examine many of the Scriptures which speak about God's concept of time.

"Beloved, be not ignorant of this one thing, that one day is with the Lord as a thousand years, and a thousand years as one day" (2 Pet. 3:8).

". . . For they shall not be ashamed that wait for me" (Isa. 49:23).

"They that wait upon the Lord shall renew their strength; they shall mount up with wings as eagles; they shall run, and not be weary; and they shall walk, and not faint" (Isa. 40:31).

Someone was telling me the other day, "I just don't understand why our house hasn't sold. I keep trying to commit it to God but I'm having such a hard time. Nothing seems to be happening."

"Do you think out of all the millions of people on the earth," I responded, "if God wanted to sell your house, He could do it? The timing must be off. Are you ready to move yet?"

The woman shook her head. "No, we're not."

"Then, you're fretting needlessly," I suggested. "God can sell it. He controls the saints as well as the sinners. He can send anybody to buy it. There's never a problem with God."

Shortly, the person realized the mistake she had made. Instead of agonizing over the situation, she began praising the Lord for His perfect time to sell the house. Sure enough, the house was sold, but only just before the new house was ready. God's timing was perfect.

Many of us tend to run ahead of God. We foolishly think God should operate according to our time schedule. Listen to the words of the Lord spoken through Isaiah.

"For my thoughts are not your thoughts, neither are your ways, my ways, saith the Lord. For as the heavens are higher than the earth, so are my ways higher than your ways, and my thoughts than your thoughts" (Isa. 55:8,9).

Back during the early 1960s, God called Tammy and myself to South America. We were attending Minneapolis Evangelistic Auditorium at the time, when Dr. Samuel Coldstone came to the church telling a marvelous story of his evangelistic endeavors in South America. He was planning to use a fancy yacht once owned by Hollywood actor Errol Flynn to sail up and down the Amazon River. His idea was to reach thousands of people living along the banks of the giant river.

Dr. Coldstone agreed that we might accompany him on the condition that we raise our own support money. Within a matter of weeks, we had raised the money but we also had discovered the true story about Dr. Coldstone. There was no yacht, nor any ministry in South America.

We now had a closed door in going to South

America. Instead of trying to force the issue, Tammy and I went into evangelism in America. Some people may have said, "We've got the money. We're going anyway." But not Jim and Tammy Bakker.

At the time, I believed God was saying no. But what would have happened had we gone? Would we have gotten a jungle disease? Would we have been killed? Only God knows.

Fifteen years later, Elmer Bueno, a veteran missionary based in Panama, was a guest on the PTL Club. As I was interviewing Elmer, the Lord spoke to me saying, "I release you to go into Latin America now."

I proposed the idea of a Spanish version of the PTL Club to Elmer with him serving as host. He immediately recognized the suggestion as from God and accepted on the spot. It was ten years ago that Elmer first felt God calling him into television ministry in Latin America but he had no means of accomplishing his goal until PTL came along.

Within a matter of weeks, PTL was producing "Club Alabare" for Central and South America. Reports are reaching us daily of the lives being changed throughout the continent.

Perhaps if I had gone to South America back in the 1960s, I could have reached several villages. But now through the medium of television, I can reach an entire continent for Jesus. Moving in God's time is what makes the difference.

After you've committed a problem to God, don't fret and fume if the answer isn't forthcoming right away. Instead, begin praising and thanking God for His perfect time. Praise will keep the burden off your back and squarely on the Lord.

At the same time, don't sit on your hands after committing a problem to God. Do something to activate your faith. If you're trying to sell a house, put an ad in the paper or hire a realtor. If you're looking for a job, send out resumes or look in the help wanted columns.

This is where your faith comes in. Follow these steps in simple faith that God will bless your actions. Act upon it. Commit the problem to God. Wait patiently on Him.

Remember this: He will bring the solution to pass.

9

A Good Confession—
Vital to the
Big Three

Many people wonder why the PTL Television Network has grown so fast. From time to time, I see people walking around the Heritage Village looking at God's abundant provision with puzzled looks on their faces. Some are actually bewildered at God's goodness. Letters and phone calls continually pose the same question, "What's the secret of all this success?"

I know PTL's incredible growth over the last three years is mind-boggling. At times, I feel as if I'm on a wild roller coaster ride.

IBM officials told me recently that PTL grows faster than their analysis can keep up with. PTL is already on the air with a Spanish version of the

PTL Club in South and Central America. Japanese and Korean editions of PTL will follow shortly. New affiliate signings occur almost daily throughout the United States. The network's rate of growth is unprecedented.

Yet how is all this being accomplished?

I believe the answer centers around the word of confession. Every time God spoke to me about a new project, I confessed that project exactly as the Lord spoke it. But I didn't just confess this in a quiet PTL board of directors meeting, nor did I casually mention it among our close friends.

Instead, I stood up on national television and announced God's plans!

As usual, many people looked amazed at my words. "But Jim, where are you going to get the money?" they always seem to ask.

My answer is always the same. "I'll get the money where I got the $5 million to pay for the Heritage Village—from God."

The PTL studios have been called the finest facilities in television. Yet PTL started the project with no money. We started during a time of recession when building contractors were going bankrupt. But God said, "build it." We committed the project to Him, spoke the words and God did the rest.

Jesus gives us a glimpse at the power of words in Mark 11:23. He says, "For verily I say unto you, That whosoever shall say unto this mountain, Be thou removed, and be thou cast into the sea; and shall not doubt in his heart, but shall believe that those things which he saith shall come to pass; he shall have whatsoever he saith."

The key words in Mark 11:23 are "say" and "saith." In order to move that mountain in your life, Jesus declares you must speak to it. The words "say," "saith" and "saying" are so important they appear over four thousand times in the King James Version of the Bible.

Without question, speech is one of the most powerful forces in the universe. God, himself, demonstrated the importance of speech by speaking creation into existence (Gen. 1:3).

Where you spend eternity is actually determined by your confession. If you receive Jesus as your Savior, it is done by confession. Romans 10:9,10 says, "That if thou shalt confess with thy mouth the Lord Jesus, and shalt believe in thine heart that God hath raised him from the dead, thou shalt be saved.

"For with the heart man believeth unto righteousness; and with the mouth confession is made unto salvation."

By the same token, Jesus said each person would be condemned by what they say. ". . . Out of thine own mouth will I judge thee . . ." (Luke 19:22).

Solomon, the wise writer of Proverbs, draws sharp attention to what's spoken in Proverbs

18:21. Says Solomon, "Death and life are in the power of the tongue. . . ."

Have You Met the Negative Family?

Have you ever been around Mr. and Mrs. Negative and their negative children? They seem to be continually standing under some black cloud.

I've seen whole families who were supposedly good Christians yet were totally negative. They're constantly in and out of the hospital. The husband has a low-paying job. He's frequently unemployed. The family can barely make ends meet financially. Something is always going wrong with Mr. and Mrs. Negative.

Even if something good does happen, the Negative family finds something bad to say about it. Their approach to life is, "Oh, well, nothing good is going to happen anyway." Everything they touch is sick just like them. Negative talk bears negative fruit.

People like Mr. and Mrs. Negative will stay under that black cloud of problems until they learn the road out of their troubles is through a positive confession. Their own confession has put them under that black cloud. But, praise God, there is a way out.

From Genesis to Revelation, the Bible demonstrates you can have victory or defeat through the confession of your lips. You can mold your own life through what you say.

Jesus said in Matthew 12:37, "For by thy words thou shalt be justified, and by thy words thou shalt be condemned."

In that same chapter, Jesus indicates a Christian can be known by the fruit of his lips just as a good tree is known by its fruit (Matt. 12:33). I actually doubt the salvation of some people because of what they say!

Doctors have learned recently that your physical body works to keep you honest by whatever you confess. If you confess fear, your body is going to produce fear. If your life is filled with complaining and bitterness, the likely result will be arthritis or cancer.

Many people speak their own doom every day. Some people have talked about their problems so much until they have come true. Not only does a negative confession damage your physical body, but it has presented a continual stumbling block to winning the world for Christ.

Joy Thieves—Relatives of the Negative Family

Mr. and Mrs. Negative have some infamous relatives, whom I call "joy thieves." They're all in the same family because the joy thieves do robbing and stealing with words.

Joy thieves are the most vicious thieves in the

whole world. They even put to shame the Brink's robbers who stole six million dollars. After all when you steal somebody's joy, you have robbed them of strength. The prophet Nehemiah said, "The joy of the Lord is your strength" (8:10).

Some people are always talking negatively about others. They backbite, gossip, slander and whisper. Did you know the Bible lists whisperers and backbiters alongside haters of God and fornicators? (Rom. 1:29-30).

Joy thieves are the kind of people who always say a new project or new idea just can't be done. Some of the joy thieves know the church is loaded with hypocrites, so why go? Other joy thieves who go to church can give you plenty of reasons why divine healing is no longer available today and they prove it by always staying sick.

Some of these joy thieves actually call themselves Christians but it's hard to tell by the way they talk and act. Without a doubt, they are the most negative people on the face of the earth.

Proverbs 6:16-19 lists seven distinct joy thieves. "There are six things which the Lord hates, yes, seven which are an abomination to Him: haughty eyes [or haughtiness], a lying tongue, and hands that shed innocent blood, a heart that devises wicked plans, feet that run rapidly to evil, a false witness who utters lies, and one who spreads strife among brothers" (NAS).

The Value of a Good Report

One of Henry Harrison's favorite Scriptures is Proverbs 15:30, "A good report maketh the bones fat." The Hebrew version of that Scripture literally says, "A good report refreshes the whole body and causes the whole body to prosper."

Unlike Mr. And Mrs. Negative or the joy thieves, who are both continually giving negative confessions and bad reports in practically every situation, Christians are supposed to give a good report all the time. "In everything give thanks: for this is the will of God in Christ Jesus concerning you" (1 Thess. 5:18).

Without question, God loves a good report from His people. Hebrews 11 has a long list of members to the Christian Hall of Fame. These are men who gave a good report (39) and who confessed they were looking for a better country (14). In some cases these heroes of faith had much worse circumstances than you or I will ever face. Yet because they gave a good report, God honored them above measure.

The three Hebrew youths—Shadrach, Meshach and Abednego—were in just such a situation according to the third chapter of Daniel. The young men had been taken captive in war and marched back to Babylon. Nebuchadnezzar, the Babylonian king, ordered everyone to bow to an image he had erected. Unless they bowed, the three Hebrews faced being burned to death in the king's fiery furnace. But listen to the good report they gave.

"If it be so, our God whom we serve is able to deliver us from the burning fiery furnace, and he will deliver us out of thine hand, O king. But if not, be it known unto thee, O king, that we will not serve thy gods, nor worship the golden image which thou hast set up" (Dan. 3:17,18).

That's what I call giving a good report in the midst of problems. The Hebrews could have looked at the flames rising from the furnace and decided to give in. That's human. Many of us would have done the same thing. But something in their hearts declared, "No. We will not bow. We will not serve."

God performed a miracle even as the three men were thrust into the flames. They were delivered unharmed and the king issued a decree reverencing their God who was able to perform such a miracle.

The story of Job presents another example of how to get out of a bad situation by giving a good report. It seems if there was ever a man who had a right to give a bad report, it was Job. When trouble came to Job's house, it came in bundles. In fact the trouble was so bad, Job's wife suggested he "curse God and die."

"But he said unto her, Thou speakest as one of the foolish women speaketh. What? shall we receive good at the hand of God, and shall we not receive evil? In all this did not Job sin with his lips" (Job 2:10).

Somehow Job was able to look beyond his bleak circumstances and trust God to work it all out. In the end, God restored all of Job's blessings and made him the most blessed man on earth at that time.

When most people hear the story of Job, they think of misery, discomfort, boils and backbiting friends. But the Scripture actually shows that Job spent more time in prosperity than trouble. Here's a sample of Job's prosperity according to Job 42:11-16.

—He had return of all his brothers and sisters.

—Every man gave him a piece of money and an earring of gold.

—He had 14,000 sheep, 6,000 camels, 1,000 yoke of oxen, and 1,000 she asses.

—He also had seven sons; three daughters who were the fairest in the land.

—And Job lived 140 more years and saw his sons and his sons' sons, even four generations.

In looking at the lives of these people—Job, the three Hebrew youths and the "heroes of faith"—there appears one common denominator. They all followed the exhortation of Hebrews 10:23, "to hold fast to our profession of faith without wavering." They confessed their faith in God. They continually gave a good report.

Winston Churchill Gives a Good Report

Winston Churchill was perhaps one of England's greatest prime ministers. His greatness was never better shown than during World War II, when England was seriously threatened by the prospect of a German invasion.

It was during this darkest and most fateful time of British history when Churchill rose in Parliament and thundered the words that both encouraged and typified the spirit of the British people:

> We shall not flag or fail. We shall fight in France, we shall fight on the seas and oceans, we shall fight with growing confidence and growing strength in the air, we shall defend our island, whatever the cost may be, we shall fight on the beaches, we shall fight on the landing grounds, we shall fight in the fields and in the streets, we shall fight in the hills; we shall never surrender.

And the British did not. The battle of Britain was won. A year later, when he spoke in the Canadian Parliament, Churchill talked about the beginning of the struggle against the Nazis:

> When I warned them [the French Government] that Britain would fight on

alone whatever they did, their Generals told their Prime Minister and his divided Cabinet: 'In three weeks England will have her neck wrung like a chicken.'
Some chicken! Some neck!

Winston Churchill knew the value of giving a good report and the powerful effects of a positive confession. If he had been a negative thinker or talker, the course of history might have been greatly altered.

The lesson is the same in the Christian life. Those who give a good report and positive confession are the ones who win the victories.

God Hates an Evil Report

Just as God loves a good report, He hates an evil one. Numbers 13 tells the story of the children of Israel preparing to cross the Jordan River and enter the promised land. But Moses first sent twelve spies into the land to bring back a report. When they returned, ten of the twelve brought back an evil report. Listen to the report in Numbers 13:27,28,32.

"And they told him, and said, We came unto the land whither thou sentest us, and surely it floweth with milk and honey; and this is the fruit of it.

"Nevertheless the people be strong that dwell in the land, and the cities are walled, and very great;

and moreover we saw the children of Anak there.

"And they brought up an evil report of the land which they had searched unto the children of Israel, saying, The land, through which we have gone to search it, is a land that eateth up the inhabitants thereof; and all the people that we saw in it are men of a great stature."

Once this evil report had been given, the children of Israel grew afraid, and wanted to return to Egypt. Look at Numbers 14:1-4.

"And all the congregation lifted up their voice, and cried; and the people wept that night. And all the children of Israel murmured against Moses and against Aaron: and the whole congregation said unto them, Would God that we had died in the land of Egypt! or would God we had died in this wilderness!

"And wherefore hath the Lord brought us unto this land, to fall by the sword, that our wives and our children should be a prey? were it not better for us to return into Egypt. And they said one to another, Let us make a captain, and let us return into Egypt."

God had performed great miracles for the children of Israel. He had shown them tremendous signs and wonders in leading them out of slavery. They actually wanted to return in spite of all God had done.

Evil reports do the same thing today as they did in Bible days. They discourage people. They kill faith. They hinder the work of God. I have known of church doors actually being closed because of evil reports, idle gossip, slander and backbiting.

Richard M. DeVos, cofounder of Amway, one of the fastest growing corporations in America, says in his book, *Believe!*, that the reason so many people let their dreams die unlived is "negative, cynical attitudes of other people."

Says DeVos, "Those other people are not enemies—they are friends, even family members. Our enemies never bother us greatly; we can usually handle them with little trouble. But our friends—if they are naysayers, constantly punching holes in our dreams with a cynical smile here, a put-down there, a constant stream of negative vibrations—our friends can kill us!"

At PTL, I have surrounded myself with men of faith. I simply won't allow myself to be surrounded by negative thinkers or talkers because they will destroy faith. Faith is a very contagious thing, just as fear is. It is easiest killed by those around us.

"Negative thoughts and attitudes feed on themselves," writes DeVos. "They pile up higher and higher until the world actually becomes the grim place that they describe."

People are always willing to point out the negatives with every situation. They have a long list of reasons why you can't achieve a certain goal. But don't listen. The people who're always telling you no generally have never achieved anything. They were afraid to try.

Even in the face of all these evil reports given to Moses, Joshua and Caleb gave a good report.

Numbers 13:30 says, "And Caleb stilled the people before Moses, and said, Let us go up at once, and possess it; for we are well able to overcome it."

Joshua and Caleb exhorted the Israelites. "And they spake unto all the company of the children of Israel, saying, The land, which we passed through to search it, is an exceeding good land. If the Lord delight in us, then he will bring us into this land, and give it us; a land which floweth with milk and honey.

"Only rebel not ye against the Lord, neither fear ye the people of the land; for they are bread for us: their defence is departed from them, and the Lord is with us: fear them not" (Num. 14:7-9).

God was upset with the spies' evil report, "I will smite them with the pestilence and disinherit them" (Num. 14:12). Those who gave the evil report died on the spot by a plague. Their children were doomed to wandering in the wilderness forty years.

Because of their good report, Joshua and Caleb were the only ones to enter the promised land. It's amazing. Joshua and Caleb saw the same things as the other ten spies. But they said, "If God is with us, then we will take the land."

That was the big difference. They weren't looking at the walled cities, the giants or their great enemies. They were looking at God, the solution to the problem. And they confessed positively.

When PTL got involved in its massive building project, I never looked at our bank balance. I kept looking at God. By faith, I even saw that beautiful Bruton Parish Church replica sitting on our empty lot. I didn't have the money to build it, but I knew God did, and that kept my confession positive.

A medical doctor recently made this statement. "You are today what you confessed yesterday." That's right in line with Proverbs 6:2, "Thou art snared with the words of thy mouth." Now is the time to plug into a good confession—the biggest Mountain Mover!

10

A New Lesson in the Big Three

PTL's annual trip to the Christian Retreat Center in Bradenton, Florida, had been planned for more than a year. It was going to be an exhausting schedule of shooting eighteen television programs in the space of one week. Some days we would be shooting three shows a day.

Some of the best known Christian personalities in the country were scheduled to be in Bradenton: Pat and Shirley Boone, Anita Bryant, Lulu Roman from "Hee Haw," Dr. C.M. Ward, the Blackwood Brothers. Three weeks of the network's time schedule were tied up in this one week. I knew if any problems occurred it would be costly to PTL.

We already had problems. Going to Florida, I knew PTL was some two million dollars behind in its bills. With 1976-1977's worst winter in history, millions of people were out of work and PTL's finances were sorely pressed. Inside of me, I had this nagging thought of impending trouble in Florida.

I had left our home in Charlotte early to spend some time in Florida before the programs would be taped. One night I awoke about two o'clock with God speaking to me.

"Jim, if you'll trust me, I am going to turn this financial crisis into victory. The devil may have meant it for harm but I am going to mean it for victory. Instead of just getting you out of the intermediate crisis, I am going to deliver PTL from its total indebtedness. Instead of just surviving the crisis, I am going to use it to bring you into victory."

Then the Lord dictated a letter for me to send to our PTL supporters explaining the situation and asking them to pray. That was Friday. Three days later, the letter was headed to some 250,000 supporters of PTL.

On Sunday, we began shooting programs in Bradenton. Like the rest of the country, Florida was experiencing an unprecedented cold snap. Palms were frozen. Much of the state's citrus crop was ruined. The grass had turned brown and

PTL's inventive staff had somehow colored it bright green.

The first I sensed we had a problem came when the Hammond organ to be used on the program wouldn't play. Then the sound system failed to operate. It was cold, and being out-of-doors the audience of some two thousand grew noticeably restless. Technicians labored over the equipment and finally—two hours late—we did the program. It was almost dark when we finished.

As I walked off the set, Roger Flessing, PTL's vice president for television, cornered me. His face was grim. "Jim, we've got a real problem on our hands," he announced tersely.

"You mean it's not just with the organ and the sound system?" I asked.

"No," he responded. "We've had a power surge and both of the RCA video tape recorders are burned out. Apparently one of the fail-safe systems did not operate properly. It looks like some of the circuits are fried to a crisp."

My heart sank like a torpedoed boat.

The thing I had greatly feared had come upon me. The worst possible thing in the whole world that could happen had happened! PTL was already two million dollars in the hole. Now my video equipment was burned out and I was hundreds of miles from the studio without any backup equipment.

My immediate reaction was to blame somebody.

Roger Flessing was the nearest person. "You probably didn't bring enough people," I snapped, "or if you had enough people, they didn't know what to do."

The situation was bleak. Spiritually, I felt as cold as the Florida climate, which was frigid. Antarctica couldn't have been colder at that moment.

Roger, a dedicated Christian man and experienced broadcasting professional, was quiet as I vented my emotions. He apparently knew I had to let off steam at somebody. "Well, there is some saving grace in the situation," he suggested positively, "although we didn't get the program taped on our recorders it was taped on a cassette recorder."

The thought of PTL being recorded on a cassette recorder bugged me even further. I had always been taught two-inch video tape was the only quality acceptable in television stations. Cassette size wouldn't do. I just knew the programs had been wasted.

"Well, that just won't do," I answered brusquely.

But Roger was more optimistic. "Well, I'm going to ship them back to Charlotte and let Jefferson Broadcasting re-dub the tapes just to see what we can get. Maybe there's something we can rescue out of this."

That same night, we taped another program at Christian Retreat and Roger Flessing decided to run the burned out machines anyway. When the tapes were received in Charlotte hours later, they had recorded the program perfectly.

How? I'll never know, since the machines hadn't been repaired yet! My only explanation is that God somehow worked a miracle for us.

The following day an emergency repairman arrived from RCA to begin working on the video machines. "I don't know how you did it," he said, shaking his head. "It's impossible to record on these machines."

"I don't know either," agreed one of PTL's technicians. "All I know is that we serve a miracle-working God. We just serve Him and He takes care of the rest."

The video machines were ultimately repaired but my troubles were far from being over. The next day after another program was taped outside in the unseasonably cold weather, Roger Flessing and Dale Hill, PTL's general manager, approached me. "Jim, we need to talk with you privately," Dale said seriously.

"Oh, no," I thought to myself. "What in the world is wrong now?"

The three of us walked away from the large crowd assembled around the PTL set and they began telling me about another financial problem facing the ministry. It seemed that PTL owed a large down payment for some equipment purchases. Our financial advisor had been attempting to reduce the size of the payment without success. Unless we have the money within twenty-four hours, the company would foreclose on us. It was an "either or" situation.

"Maybe we ought to just give up," I responded wearily as this new problem was explained. "This thing is getting so big. PTL is going all over the world. It takes over a million and a half dollars a month just to stay on the air. I'm not a businessman. I'm a preacher."

Both men shook their heads. "No," they said almost simultaneously.

"Jim, we're going to make it somehow," Dale said confidently. "We're going to stick together and beat this thing."

"That's right," Roger agreed. "We can do it."

Roger and Dale's faith helped mine. But this was still another mountain that had to be moved. I had faced huge ones before but this mountain looked like the biggest I had ever seen.

My letter to PTL's partners had gone out on Monday but it was too early to know its response—so the big $2 million debt was still looking me in the eyes. Now I had an immediate need of $85,000 or I faced the terrible prospect of losing some valuable equipment.

That night, we taped another program. Demos Shakarian, founder and president of the Full Gospel Business Men's Fellowship International (FGBMFI) had flown in from Los Angeles especially for the program. As he spoke to the crowd, faith began to build in my heart.

He told the thrilling story of how his family had been miraculously spared when their village in Armenia had been wiped out by war. He talked about the seemingly endless string of miracles God had performed in the lives of the Shakarian family in getting them safely to America. He talked about hearing the voice of God and following Him.

The more Demos Shakarian spoke, the more faith began to grow and expand inside of me. My mountains began to look smaller already. God began to look more than able to handle the situation.

Near the end of the program, I shared with the audience something of the problem PTL was currently facing. Without planning to do so, I began confessing, "In twenty-four hours, we're going to have that $85,000."

"I don't know how God is going to do it," I told the audience. "I only know He will."

Nancy Harmon and her singing group, "The Victory Voices," and Dr. Evelyn Carter, a popular black preacher, were guests on the program that night. The Lord reminded me Nancy and her group had a need. They were currently traveling around the country in a van that looked like a converted bread truck. The van was so poorly equipped several members of the group even had to sit on crates as they traveled.

PTL had a beautiful motor coach we were using as a crew bus for remote broadcasts. The Lord impressed me to give the bus to Nancy and her singing group. In obedience and faith, I did.

But the Lord wasn't finished. "Rev. Ev"—Dr. Evelyn Carter—needed transportation too. In fact, her pastor had written me earlier that she was in desperate need of a car. The Lord told me to give "Rev. Ev" my personal car, a Cadillac, which He had so bountifully supplied months before. Once again in faith, I did.

As I gave in obedience to the Lord, something began happening. The giving—that explosive force in commitment—triggered a reaction.

When the program ended, people began coming up to shake my hand. As the people surged forward, they were leaving checks or money in my hands. Many were giving hundred dollar bills. The father of a PTL staff member gave $4,000. A businessman gave $10,000.

When the last of the people had finished greeting me, I had over $36,000 in my hands. What a miracle! I could sense God was beginning to move my mountain. Thirty-six thousand dollars is a lot of money but I needed $85,000.

The next morning, I went to the auditorium where Tammy was hosting a program. All the while, the devil was whispering in my ear. "You are a fool. You will never make it this time. You are a fool."

Somehow I was moving in faith though. I explained some of the details to the audience. Once again, I confessed, "I know before the service tonight, we're going to have the $85,000."

That afternoon I called our offices in Charlotte and discovered we had an additional $22,000 available to send to the company demanding payment. We now had $58,000.

All day long, people continued shaking my hand and pressing money into my palm. The cafeteria crew at Christian Retreat chipped in a thousand dollars. Gerald Derstine, president of the Retreat, reminded me an offering had been taken earlier for PTL. Someone counted the money and found it was $2,000.

By now, my faith was leaping and growing because the hand of God was moving everywhere I looked. That mountain of financial debt was looking smaller and smaller.

Hours later, I walked back into the auditorium for the nightly service where I had so boldly proclaimed we would have the money. "Have you made it yet?" people in the crowd shouted. Their faith seemed to be growing too.

I explained we hadn't received all the money we needed. Everybody seemed to want to wait on God to supply the money before the program began. So, we just began singing and praising the Lord. After a while nobody was thinking about the money, we were so caught up in praising God.

But within ten minutes, donations totaling over $25,000 had been brought to the platform. God had supplied abundantly. We had actually gone over the goal of $85,000. The victory had been won!

Not only did God provide the $85,000 in twenty-four hours but the next day I received word that PTL had received twenty-seven trays of mail. (A tray contains 500 letters.) Our record mail delivery had been fourteen trays before. The following day, thirty-nine trays of mail came. With the mail came hundreds of thousands of dollars in contributions to help PTL over the financial crisis. Ultimately two million dollars would be donated to the ministry paying all the outstanding bills.

Through the month called "the coldest in U.S. history," through great national calamities of weather, PTL had the largest financial month in its entire history. It fulfilled completely what God told me in the beginning. The crisis was for our good, not our harm.

Romans 8:28 had been proven again. "And we know that all things work together for good to them that love God, to them who are the called according to his purpose." Praise God.

What My Experience Taught Me

The Christian life is a learning experience and I'm no different than anybody else in that regard.

I'm still learning. And through this tremendous experience of double-barrel financial trouble, I have learned some new lessons in practicing the Big Three.

One of the most important lessons I learned involves the suggestions of the devil. He had been whispering to me all along about bad things happening to PTL while in Florida. Instead of chasing him off with the word of God, I listened. I bought his suggestions.

On top of that, I didn't get the devilish thoughts out of my mind. They rolled over and over. Before long, the devil had me wondering what bad thoughts would actually happen. What a trap!

From this episode, I have learned not to buy the suggestions of the devil. Jim Bakker—just like everybody else—must continue to defeat the devil in his mind.

Secondly, I knew PTL was in the center of God's will. This is very important for every child of God. No matter how rotten the problems or how stiff the opposition, I knew God would take care of us. God would provide. He would not abandon us.

As never before, I realized God can be trusted. This understanding of God, I found, is absolutely basic to the Christian life.

Thirdly, I learned praise is an act of the will. During the week before we saw any victory in the financial problems and when the technical woes were still upon us, we began freely praising the

Lord in one of our services. We praised and worshiped God even though many of us didn't feel like it. In fact that night I wanted to leave the room and just cry.

You and I have a will that God won't violate. We can praise Him through the trouble and trials, or we can grumble and complain about the situation. We praised God and the victory ultimately came.

Are you in a similar situation? Maybe it's time you started praising God. I've found the "praise route" is the easiest way out of trouble.

Fourthly, I gave even though PTL was in need itself. We committed the problem to God and we acted in faith. In this case, I gave things that were valuable to me—a motor coach to Nancy Harmon and her singing group and my own personal car to Dr. Evelyn Carter.

I gave the vehicles in acting out our trust, our basic raw-bone commitment to God. I obeyed God. That was faith in action. In response, God gave PTL a tremendous miracle.

Naturally, I don't believe it was just one thing that moved the hand of God. It was all of these facets to the Big Three Mountain-Movers working together.

The miracle wasn't all Jim Bakker either. Roger Flessing and Dale Hill were instrumental in getting me over the discouragement. They reminded me God would work everything out. I had my eyes temporarily on the problem, not

God, the problem-solver.

Once again, I have been reminded God has the answer to the problems Jim Bakker faces. He also has the answers to your problems. Moving mountains is the most exciting way to live. I pray you have already decided to make mountain-moving a life style too.